THE KING'S JACKAL

He Swung the Crown Prince High Upon His Shoulder.

THE KING'S JACKAL

BY

RICHARD HARDING DAVIS

WITH ILLUSTRATIONS BY

Charles Dana Gibson

CHARLES SCRIBNER'S SONS
NEW YORK:::::::::::::::::: 1905

CONTENTS

ILLUSTRATIONS

THE KING'S JACKAL

The King's Jackal

I

THE private terrace of the Hotel Grand
Bretagne, at Tangier, was shaded by a
great awning of red and green and yellow, and
strewn with colored mats, and plants in pots, and
wicker chairs. It reached out from the King's
apartments into the Garden of Palms, and was
hidden by them on two sides, and showed from
the third the blue waters of the Mediterranean
and the great shadow of Gibraltar in the distance.

The Sultan of Morocco had given orders from
Fez that the King of Messina, in spite of his in-
cognito, should be treated during his stay in Tangier with the consideration due to his rank, so one-
half of the Hotel Grand Bretagne had been set
aside for him and his suite, and two soldiers of
the Bashaw's Guard sat outside of his door with
drawn swords. They were answerable with their
heads for the life and safety of the Sultan's guest,
and as they could speak no language but their own,

3

they made a visit to his Majesty more a matter
of adventure than of etiquette.

Niccolas, the King's major-domo, stepped out
upon the terrace and swept the Mediterranean
with a field-glass for the third time since sunrise.
He lowered it, and turned doubtfully toward the
two soldiers.

"The boat from Gibraltar—has she arrived
yet?" he asked.

The two ebony figures shook their heads stiffly,
as though they resented this introduction of a
foreign language, and continued to shake their
heads as the servant addressed the same question
to them in a succession of strange tongues.

"Well," said Colonel Erhaupt, briskly, as he
followed Niccolas out upon the terrace, "has the
boat arrived? And the launch from the yacht,"
he continued, "has it started for shore yet?"

The man pointed to where the yacht lay, a mile
outside the harbor, and handed him the glass.

"It is but just now leaving the ship's side," he
said. "But I cannot make out who comes in her.
Ah, pardon," he added quickly, as he pointed to
a stout elderly gentleman who walked rapidly
toward them through the garden. "The Gibraltar boat must be in, sir. Here is Baron Barrat
coming up the path."

The King's Jackal

Colonel Erhaupt gave an exclamation of satisfaction, and waved his hand to the newcomer in welcome.

"Go tell his Majesty," he said to the servant.

The man hesitated and bowed. "His Majesty still sleeps."

"Wake him," commanded Erhaupt. "Tell him I said to do so. Well, Baron," he cried, gayly, as he stepped forward, "welcome—or are you welcome?" he added, with an uneasy laugh.

"I should be. I have succeeded," the other replied gruffly, as he brushed past him. "Where is the King?"

"He will be here in a moment. I have sent to wake him. And you have been successful? Good. I congratulate you. How far successful?"

The Baron threw himself into one of the wicker chairs, and clapped his hands impatiently for a servant. "Twelve thousand pounds in all," he replied. "That's more than he expected. It was like pulling teeth at first. I want some coffee at once," he said to the attendant, "and a bath. That boat reeked with Moors and cattle, and there was no wagon-lit on the train from Madrid. I sat up all night, and played cards with that young Cellini. Have Madame Zara and Kalonay

5

returned? I see the yacht in the harbor. **Did** she succeed?"

"We do not know; the boat only arrived at daybreak. They are probably on the launch that is coming in now."

As Barrat sipped his coffee and munched his rolls with the silent energy of a hungry man, the Colonel turned and strode up and down the terrace, pulling at his mustache and glancing sideways. When the Baron had lighted a cigarette and thrown himself back in his chair, Erhaupt halted and surveyed him in some anxiety.

"You have been gone over two weeks," he said.

"I should like to see you accomplish as much in as short a time," growled the other. "You know Paris. You know how hard it is to get people to be serious there. I had the devil's own time at first. You got my cablegram?"

"Yes; it wasn't encouraging."

"Well, I wasn't hopeful myself. They wouldn't believe a word of it at first. They said Louis hadn't shown such great love for his country or his people since his exile that they could feel any confidence in him, and that his conduct in the last six years did not warrant their joining any undertaking in which he was concerned. You can't blame them. They've backed him so many times

already, and they've been bitten, and they're shy,
naturally. But I swore he was repentant, that he
saw the error of his ways, that he wanted to sit
once more before he died on the throne of his
ancestors, and that he felt it was due to his son
that he should make an effort to get him back his
birthright. It was the son won them. 'Exhibit
A,' I call him. None of them would hear of it
until I spoke of the Prince. So when I saw that,
I told them he was a fine little chap, healthy and
manly and brave, and devoted to his priest, and
all that rot, and they began to listen. At first they
wanted his Majesty to abdicate, and give the boy
a clear road to the crown, but of course I hushed
that up. I told them we were acting advisedly,
that we had reason to know that the common
people of Messina were sick of the Republic, and
wanted their King; that Louis loved the common
people like a father; that he would re-establish the
Church in all her power, and that Father Paul was
working day and night for us, and that the Vati-
can was behind us. Then I dealt out decorations
and a few titles, which Louis has made smell so
confoundedly rank to Heaven that nobody would
take them. It was like a game. I played one
noble gentleman against another, and gave this
one a portrait of the King one day, and the other

a miniature of 'Exhibit A' the next, and they grew jealous, and met together, and talked it over, and finally unlocked their pockets. They contributed about £9,000 between them. Then the enthusiasm spread to the women, and they gave me their jewels, and a lot of youngsters volunteered for the expedition, and six of them came on with me in the train last night. I won two thousand francs from that boy Cellini on the way down. They're all staying at the Continental. I promised them an audience this morning."

"Good," commented the Colonel, "good— £9,000. I suppose you took out your commission in advance?"

"I took out nothing," returned the other, angrily. "I brought it all with me, and I have a letter from each of them stating just what he or she subscribed toward the expedition,—the Duke Dantiz, so much; the Duke D'Orvay, 50,000 francs; the Countess Mattini, a diamond necklace. It is all quite regular. I played fair."

The Colonel had stopped in his walk, and had been peering eagerly down the leafy path through the garden. "Is that not Zara coming now?" he asked. "Look, your eyes are better than mine."

Barrat rose quickly, and the two men walked

8

forward, and bowed with the easy courtesy of old
comrades to a tall, fair girl who came hurriedly up
the steps. The Countess Zara was a young woman,
but one who had stood so long on guard against
the world, that the strain had told, and her eyes
were hard and untrustful, so that she looked much
older than she really was. Her life was of two
parts. There was little to be told of the first part;
she was an English girl who had come from a
manufacturing town to study art and live alone in
Paris, where she had been too indolent to work,
and too brilliant to remain long without companions eager for her society. Through them and
the stories of her wit and her beauty, she had come
to know the King of Messina, and with that meeting the second part of her life began; for she had
found something so attractive, either in his title
or in the cynical humor of the man himself, that
for the last two years she had followed his fortunes, and Miss Muriel Winter, art student, had
become the Countess Zara, and an uncrowned
queen. She was beautiful, with great masses of
yellow hair and wonderful brown eyes. Her manner when she spoke seemed to show that she despised the world and those in it almost as thoroughly as she despised herself.

On the morning of her return from Messina,

she wore a blue serge yachting suit with a golf cloak hanging from her shoulders, and as she crossed the terrace she pulled nervously at her gloves and held out her hand covered with jewels to each of the two men.

"I bring good news," she said, with an excited laugh. "Where is Louis?"

"I will tell his Majesty that you have come. You are most welcome," the Baron answered.

But as he turned to the door it opened from the inside and the King came toward them, shivering and blinking his eyes in the bright sunlight. It showed the wrinkles and creases around his mouth and the blue veins under the mottled skin, and the tiny lines at the corners of his little bloodshot eyes that marked the pace at which he had lived as truthfully as the rings on a tree-trunk tell of its quiet growth.

He caught up his long dressing-gown across his chest as though it were a mantle, and with a quick glance to see that there were no other witnesses to his déshabillé, bent and kissed the woman's hand, and taking it in his own stroked it gently.

"My dear Marie," he lisped, "it is like heaven to have you back with us again. We have felt your absence every hour. Pray be seated, and pardon my robe. I saw you through the blinds and

immovable as blind beggars before a mosque. "Do they understand?" she asked.

"No," the King assured her. "They understand nothing, but that they are to keep people away from me—and they do it very well. I wish I could import them to Paris to help Niccolas fight off creditors. Continue, we are most impatient."

"We left here last Sunday night, as you know," she said. "We passed Algiers the next morning and arrived off the island at mid-day, anchoring outside in the harbor. We flew the Royal Yacht Squadron's pennant, and an owner's private signal that we invented on the way down. They sent me ashore in a boat, and Kalonay and Father Paul continued on along the southern shore, where they have been making speeches in all the coast-towns and exciting the people in favor of the revolution. I heard of them often while I was at the capital, but not from them. The President sent a company of carbineers to arrest them the very night they returned and smuggled me on board the yacht again. We put off as soon as I came over the side and sailed directly here.

"As soon as I landed on Tuesday I went to the Hôtel de Messina, and sent my card to the President. He is that man Palaccio, the hotel-keeper's son, the man you sent out of the country for writing pamphlets against the monarchy, and who lived in Sicily during his exile. He gave me an audience at once, and I told my story. As he knew who I was, I explained that I had quarrelled with you, and that I was now prepared to sell him the secrets of an expedition which you were fitting out with the object of re-establishing yourself on the throne. He wouldn't believe that there was any such expedition, and said it was blackmail, and threatened to give me to the police if I did not leave the island in twenty-four hours—he was exceedingly rude. So I showed him receipts for ammunition and rifles and Maxim guns, and copies of the oath of allegiance to the expedition, and papers of the yacht, in which she was described as an armored cruiser, and he rapidly grew polite, even humble, and I made him apologize first, and then take me out to luncheon. That was the first day. The second day telegrams began to come in from the coast-towns, saying that the Prince Kalonay and Father Paul were preaching and exciting the people to rebellion, and travelling from town to town in a man-of-war. Then he was frightened. The Prince with his popularity in the south was alarming enough, but the Prince and Father Superior to help him seemed to mean the end of the Republic.

The King's Jackal

"I learned while I was down there that the people think the father put some sort of a ban on every one who had anything to do with driving the Dominican monks out of the island and with the destruction of the monasteries. I don't know whether he did or not, but they believe he did, which is the same thing, and that superstitious little beast, the President, certainly believed it; he attributed everything that had gone wrong on the island to that cause. Why, if a second cousin of the wife of a brother of one of the men who helped to fire a church falls off his horse and breaks his leg they say that he is under the curse of the Father Superior, and there are many who believe the Republic will never succeed until Paul returns and the Church is re-established. The Government seems to have kept itself well informed about your Majesty's movements, and it has never felt any anxiety that you would attempt to return, and it did not fear the Church party because it knew that without you the priests could do nothing. But when Paul, whom the common people look upon as a living saint and martyr, returned hand in hand with your man Friday, they were in a panic and felt sure the end had come. So the President called a hasty meeting of his Cabinet. And such a Cabinet! I wish you could have seen them, Louis, with me in the centre playing on them like an advocate before a jury. They were the most dreadful men I ever met, bourgeois and stupid and ugly to a degree. Two of them were commission-merchants, and one of them is old Dr. Gustavanni, who kept the chemist's shop in the Piazza Royale. They were quite silly with fear, and they begged me to tell them how they could avert the fall of the Republic and prevent your landing. And I said that it was entirely a question of money; that if we were paid sufficiently the expedition would not land and we would leave them in peace, but that——"

The King shifted his legs uneasily, and coughed behind his thin, pink fingers.

"That was rather indiscreet, was it not, Marie?" he murmured. "The idea was to make them think that I, at least, was sincere; was not that it? To make it appear that though there were traitors in his camp, the King was in most desperate earnest? If they believe that, you see, it will allow me to raise another expedition as soon as the money we get for this one is gone; but if you have let them know that I am the one who is selling out, you have killed the goose that lays the golden eggs. They will never believe us when we cry wolf again——"

The King's Jackal

"You must let me finish," Zara interrupted. "I did not involve you in the least. I said that there were traitors in the camp of whom I was the envoy, and that if they would pay us 300,000 francs we would promise to allow the expedition only to leave the yacht. Their troops could then make a show of attacking our landing-party and we would raise the cry of 'treachery' and retreat to the boats. By this we would accomplish two things,—we would satisfy those who had contributed funds toward the expedition that we had at least made an honest effort, and your Majesty would be discouraged by such treachery from ever attempting another attack. The money was to be paid two weeks later in Paris, to me or to whoever brings this ring that I wear. The plan we finally agreed upon is this: The yacht is to anchor off Basnai next Thursday night. At high tide, which is just about daybreak, we are to lower our boats and land our men on that long beach to the south of the breakwater. The troops of the Republic are to lie hidden in the rocks until our men have formed. Then they are to fire over their heads, and we are to retreat in great confusion, return to the yacht, and sail away. Two weeks later they are to pay the money into my hands, or," she added, with a smile, as she held up her fourth finger, "to whoever brings this ring. And I need not say that the ring will not leave my finger."

There was a moment's pause, as though the men were waiting to learn if she had more to tell, and then the King threw back his head and laughed softly. He saw Erhaupt's face above his shoulder, filled with the amazement and indignation of a man who as a duellist and as a soldier had shown a certain brute courage, and the King laughed again.

"What do you think of that, Colonel?" he cried, gayly. "They are a noble race, my late subjects."

"Bah!" exclaimed the German. "I didn't know we were dealing with a home for old women."

The Baron laughed comfortably. "It is like taking money from a blind beggar's hat," he said.

"Why, with two hundred men that I could pick up in London," Erhaupt declared, contemptuously, "I would guarantee to put you on the throne in a fortnight."

"Heaven forbid!" exclaimed his Majesty. "So they surrendered as quickly as that, did they?" he asked, nodding toward Madame Zara to continue.

The Countess glanced again over her shoulder and bit her lips in some chagrin. Her eyes showed her disappointment. "It may seem an easy victory to you," she said, consciously, "but I doubt, knowing all the circumstances, if any of your Majesty's

gentlemen could have served you as well. It
needed a woman and——"

"It needed a beautiful woman," interrupted the
King, quickly, in a tone that he would have used
to a spoiled child. "It needed a woman of tact, a
woman of courage, a woman among women—the
Countess Zara. Do not imagine, Marie, that we
undervalue your part. It is their lack of courage
that distresses Colonel Erhaupt."

"One of them, it is true, did wish to fight," the
Countess continued, with a smile; "a Frenchman
named Renauld, whom they have put in charge of
the army. He scoffed at the whole expedition, but
they told him that a foreigner could not understand as they did the danger of the popularity of
the Prince Kolonay, who, by a speech or two
among the shepherds and fishermen, could raise an
army."

The King snapped his fingers impatiently.

"An army of brigands and smugglers!" he exclaimed. "That for his popularity!" But he instantly raised his hands as though in protest at
his own warmth of speech and in apology for his
outbreak.

"His zeal will ruin us in time. He is deucedly
in the way," he continued, in his usual tone of easy
cynicism. "We should have let him into our plans

from the first, and then if he chose to take no part in them we would at least have had a free hand. As it is now, we have three different people to deceive: this Cabinet of shopkeepers, which seems easy enough; Father Paul and his fanatics of the Church party; and this apostle of the divine right of kings, Kalonay. And he and the good father are not fools——"

At these words Madame Zara glanced again toward the garden, and this time with such evident uneasiness in her face that Barrat eyed her with quick suspicion.

"What is it?" he asked, sharply. "There is something you have not told us."

The woman looked at the King, and he nodded his head as though in assent. "I had to tell them who else was in the plot besides myself," she said, speaking rapidly. "I had to give them the name of some man who they knew would be able to do what I have promised we could do—who could put a stop to the revolution. The name I gave was his —Kalonay's."

Barrat threw himself forward in his chair.

"Kalonay's?" he cried, incredulously.

"Kalonay's?" echoed Erhaupt. "What madness, Madame! Why name the only one who is sincere?"

The King's Jackal

"She will explain," said the King, in an uneasy voice; "let her explain. She has acted according to my orders and for the best, but I confess I——"

"Some one had to be sacrificed," returned the woman, boldly, "and why not he? Indeed, if we wish to save ourselves, there is every reason that it should be he. You know how mad he is for the King's return, how he himself wishes to get back to the island and to his old position there. Why, God only knows, but it is so. What pleasure he finds in a land of mists and fogs, in a ruined castle with poachers and smuggling fishermen for companions, I cannot comprehend. But the fact remains, he always speaks of it as home and he wishes to return. And now, suppose he learns the truth, as he may at any moment, and discovers that the whole expedition for which he is staking his soul and life is a trick, a farce; that we use it only as a bait to draw money from the old nobility, and to frighten the Republic into paying us to leave them in peace? How do we know what he might not do? He may tell the whole of Europe. He may turn on you and expose you, and then what have we left? It is your last chance. It is our last chance. We have tried everything else, and we cannot show ourselves in Europe, at least not without money in our hands. But by naming Kalonay

The King's Jackal

I have managed it so that we have only to show the written agreement I have made with the Republic and he is silenced. In it they have promised to pay the Prince Kalonay, naming him in full, 300,000 francs if the expedition is withdrawn. That agreement is in my hands, and that is our answer to whatever he may think or say. Our word is as good as his, or as bad; we are all of the same party as far as Europe cares, and it becomes a falling out among thieves, and we are equal."

Baron Barrat leaned forward and marked each word with a movement of his hand.

"Do I understand you to say," he asked, "that you have a paper signed by the Republic agreeing to pay 300,000 francs to Kalonay? Then how are we to get it?" he demanded, incredulously. "From him?"

"It is made payable to him," continued the woman, "or to whoever brings this ring I wear to the banking-house of the Schlevingens two weeks after the expedition has left the island. I explained that clause to them by saying that Kalonay and I were working together against the King, and as he might be suspicious if we were both to leave him so soon after the failure of the expedition we would be satisfied if they gave the money to whichever one first presented the ring. Suppose

I had said," she went on, turning to the King, "that it was either Barrat or the Colonel here who had turned traitor. They know the Baron of old, when he was Chamberlain and ran your roulette wheel at the palace. They know he is not the man to turn back an expedition. And the Colonel, if he will pardon me, has sold his services so often to one side or another that it would have been difficult to make them believe that this time he is sincere. But Kalonay, the man they fear most next to your Majesty—to have him turn traitor, why, that was a master stroke. Even those boors, stupid as they are, saw that. When they made out the agreement they put down all his titles, and laughed as they wrote them in. 'Prince Judas' they called him, and they were in ecstasies at the idea of the aristocrat suing for blood-money against his sovereign, of the man they feared showing himself to be only a common blackmailer. It delighted them to find a prince royal sunk lower than themselves, this man who has treated them like curs—like the curs they are," she broke out suddenly—"like the curs they are!"

She rose and laughed uneasily as though at her own vehemence.

"I am tired," she said, avoiding the King's eyes; "the trip has tired me. If you will excuse me, I

will go to my rooms—through your hall-way, if
I may."

"Most certainly," said the King. "I trust you
will be rested by dinner-time. Au revoir, my fair
ambassadrice."

The woman nodded and smiled back at him
brightly, and Louis continued to look after her
as she disappeared down the corridor. He rubbed
the back of his fingers across his lips, and thoughtfully examined his finger-nails.

"I wonder," he said, after a pause, looking up
at Barrat. The Baron raised his eyebrows with a
glance of polite interrogation.

"I wonder if Kalonay dared to make love to
her on the way down."

The Baron's face became as expressionless as a
death-mask, and he shrugged his shoulders in protest.

"—Or did she make love to Kalonay?" the
King insisted, laughing gently. "I wonder now.
I do not care to know, but I wonder."

According to tradition the Kalonay family was
an older one than that of the House of Artois, and
its name had always been the one next in importance to that of the reigning house. The history
of Messina showed that different members of the
Kalonay family had fought and died for different

kings of Artois, and had enjoyed their favor and shared their reverses with equal dignity, and that they had stood like a rampart when the kingdom was invaded by the levelling doctrines of Republicanism and equality. And though the Kalonays were men of stouter stuff than their cousins of Artois, they had never tried to usurp their place, but had set an example to the humblest shepherd of unfailing loyalty and good-will to the King and his lady. The Prince Kalonay, who had accompanied the Dominican monk to Messina, was the last of his race, and when Louis IV. had been driven off the island, he had followed his sovereign into exile as a matter of course, and with his customary good-humor. His estates, in consequence of this step, had been taken up by the Republic, and Kalonay had accepted the loss philosophically as the price one pays for loving a king. He found exile easy to bear in Paris, and especially so as he had never relinquished the idea that some day the King would return to his own again. So firmly did he believe in this, and so keenly was his heart set upon it, that Louis had never dared to let him know that for himself exile in Paris and the Riviera was vastly to be preferred to authority over a rocky island hung with fogs, and inhabited by dull merchants and fierce banditti.

The King's Jackal

The conduct of the King during their residence in Paris would have tried the loyalty of one less gay and careless than Kalonay, for he was a sorry monarch, and if the principle that "the King can do no wrong" had not been bred in the young Prince's mind, he would have deserted his sovereign in the early days of their exile. But as it was, he made excuses for him to others and to himself, and served the King's idle purposes so well that he gained for himself the name of the King's Jackal, and there were some who regarded him as little better than the King's confidential blackguard, and man Friday, the weakest if the most charming of his court of adventurers.

At the first hint which the King gave of his desire to place himself again in power, Kalonay had ceased to be his Jackal and would have issued forth as a commander-in-chief, had the King permitted him; but it was not to Louis's purpose that the Prince should know the real object of the expedition, so he assigned its preparation to Erhaupt, and despatched Kalonay to the south of the island. At the same time Madame Zara had been sent to the north of the island, ostensibly to sound the sentiment of the old nobility, but in reality to make capital out of the presence there of Kalonay and Father Paul.

The King's Jackal

The King rose hurriedly when the slim figure of
the Prince and the broad shoulders and tonsured
head of the monk appeared at the farthest end of
the garden-walk.

"They are coming!" he cried, with a guilty
chuckle; "so I shall run away and finish dressing.
I leave you to receive the first shock of Kalonay's
enthusiasm alone. I confess he bores me. Remember, the story Madame Zara told them in the
yacht is the one she told us this morning, that none
of the old royalists at the capital would promise us any assistance. Be careful now, and play
your parts prettily. We are all terribly in earnest."

Kalonay's enthusiasm had not spent itself entirely before the King returned. He had still a
number of amusing stories to tell, and he reviewed
the adventures of the monk and himself with such
vivacity and humor that the King nodded his head
in delight, and even the priest smiled indulgently
at the recollection.

Kalonay had seated himself on one of the tables,
with his feet on a chair and with a cigarette burning between his fingers. He was a handsome, dark
young man of thirty, with the impulsive manner of
a boy. Dissipation had left no trace on his face,
and his eyes were as innocent of evil and as beauti-

ful as a girl's, and as eloquent as his tongue. "May
the Maria Santissima pity the girls they look
upon," his old Spanish nurse used to say of them.
But Kalonay had shown pity for every one save
himself. His training at an English public school,
and later as a soldier in the École Polytechnique
at Paris, had saved him from a too early fall, and
men liked him instinctively, and the women much
too well.

"It was good to be back there again," he cried,
with a happy sigh. "It was good to see the clouds
following each other across the old mountains and
throwing black shadows on the campagna, and to
hear the people's patois and to taste Messinian
wine again and to know it was from your own hillside. All our old keepers came down to the coast
to meet us, and told me about the stag-hunt the
week before, and who was married, and who was in
jail, and who had been hanged for shooting a cus-
toms officer, and they promised fine deer stalking
if I get back before the snow leaves the ridges, for
they say the deer have not been hunted and are
running wild." He stopped and laughed. "I for-
got," he said, "your Majesty does not care for the
rude pleasures of my half of the island." Kalonay
threw away his cigarette, clasping his hands before
him with a sudden change of manner.

The King's Jackal

"But seriously," he cried, "as I have been telling them—I wish your Majesty could have heard the offers they made us, and could have seen the tears running down their faces when we assured them that you would return. I wished a thousand times that we had brought you with us. With you at our head we can sweep the island from one end to the other. We will gather strength and force as we go, as a landslide grows, and when we reach the capital we will strike it like a human avalanche.

"And I wish you could have heard him speak," Kalonay cried, his enthusiasm rising as he turned and pointed with his hand at the priest. "There is the leader! He made my blood turn hot with his speeches, and when he had finished I used to find myself standing on my tiptoes and shouting with the rest. Without him I could have done nothing. They knew me too well; but the laziest rascals in the village came to welcome him again, and the women and men wept before him and brought their children to be blessed, and fell on their knees and kissed his sandals. It was like the stories they tell you when you are a child. He made us sob with regret and he filled us with fresh resolves. Oh, it is very well for you to smile, you old cynics," he cried, smiling at his own fervor, "but I tell you, I have lived since I saw you last!"

The priest stood silent with his hands hidden inside his great sleeves, and his head rising erect and rigid from his cowl. The eyes of the men were turned upon him curiously, and he glanced from one to the other, as though mistrusting their sympathy.

"It was not me—it was the Church they came to welcome. The fools," he cried bitterly, "they thought they could destroy the faith of the people by banishing the servants of the Church. As soon end a mother's love for her children by putting an ocean between them. For six years those peasants have been true. I left them faithful, I returned to find them faithful. And now—" he concluded, looking steadily at the King as though to hold him to account, "and now they are to have their reward."

The King bowed his head gravely in assent. "They are to have their reward," he repeated. He rose and with a wave of his hand invited the priest to follow him, and they walked together to the other end of the terrace. When they were out of hearing of the others the King seated himself, and the priest halted beside his chair.

"I wish to speak with you, father," Louis said,

The King's Jackal

"concerning this young American girl, Miss Carson, who has promised to help us—to help you—with her money. Has she said yet how much she means to give us," asked the King, "and when she means to let us have it? It is a delicate matter, and I do not wish to urge the lady, but we are really greatly in need of money. Baron Barrat, who arrived from Paris this morning, brings back no substantial aid, although the sympathy of the old nobility, he assures me, is with us. Sympathy, however, does not purchase Maxim guns, nor pay for rations, and Madame Zara's visit to the capital was, as you know, even less successful."

"Your Majesty has seen Miss Carson, then?" the priest asked.

"Yes, her mother and she have been staying at the Continental ever since they followed you here from Paris, and I have seen her once or twice during your absence. The young lady seems an earnest daughter of our faith, and she is deeply in sympathy with our effort to re-establish your order and the influence of the Church upon the island. I have explained to her that the only way in which the Church can regain her footing there is through my return to the throne, and Miss Carson has hinted that she is willing to make even a larger contribution than the one she first mentioned. If she means to do this, it would be well if she did it at once."

"Perhaps I have misunderstood her," said the priest, after a moment's consideration; "but I thought the sum she meant to contribute was to be given only after the monarchy has been formally established, and that she wished whatever she gave to be used exclusively in rebuilding the churches and the monastery. I do not grudge it to your Majesty's purpose, but so I understood her."

"Ah, that is quite possible," returned Louis, easily; "it may be that she did so intend at first, but since I have talked with her she has shown a willing disposition to aid us not only later, but now. My success means your success," he continued, smiling pleasantly as he rose to his feet, "so I trust you will urge her to be prompt. She seems to have unlimited resources in her own right. Do you happen to know from whence her money comes?"

"Her mother told me," said the priest, "that Mr. Carson before his death owned mines and railroads. They live in California, near the Mission of Saint Francis. I have written concerning them to the Father Superior there, and he tells me that Mr. Carson died a very rich man, and that he was a generous servant of the Church. His daughter has but just inherited her father's fortune, and her one idea of using it is to give it to the Church, as he would have done."

The priest paused and seemed to consider what the King had just told him. "I will speak with her," he said, "and ask her aid as fully as she can give it. May I inquire how far your Majesty has taken her into our plans?"

"Miss Carson is fully informed," the King replied briefly. "And if you wish to speak with her you can see her now; she and her mother are coming to breakfast with me to hear the account of your visit to the island. You can speak with her then—and, father," the King added, lowering his eyes and fingering the loose sleeve of the priest's robe, "it would be well, I think, to have this presentation of the young nobles immediately after the luncheon, while Miss Carson is still present. We might even make a little ceremony of it, and so show her that she is fully in our confidence—that she is one of our most valued supporters. It might perhaps quicken her interest in the cause."

"I see no reason why that should not be," said the priest, thoughtfully, turning his eyes to the sea below them. "Madame Zara," he added, without moving his eyes, "will not be present."

The Monk Continued to Gaze Steadily at the Blue Waters.

The King's Jackal

The King straightened himself slightly, and for a brief moment of time looked at the priest in silence, but the monk continued to gaze steadily at the blue waters.

"Madame Zara will not be present," the King repeated, coldly.

"There are a few fishermen and mountaineers, your Majesty," the priest continued, turning an unconscious countenance to the King, "who came back with us from the island. They come as a deputation to inform your Majesty of the welcome that waits you, and I have promised them an audience. If you will pardon me I would suggest that you receive these honest people at the same time with the others, and that his Highness the Crown Prince be also present, and that he receive them with you. Their anxiety to see him is only second to their desire to speak to your Majesty. You will find some of your most loyal subjects among these men. Their forefathers have been faithful to your house and to the Church for many generations."

"Excellent," said the King; "I shall receive them immediately after the deputation from Paris. Consult with Baron Barrat and Kalonay, please, about the details. I wish either Kalonay or yourself to make the presentation. I see Miss Carson and her mother coming. After luncheon, then, at, say, three o'clock—will that be satisfactory?"

"As your Majesty pleases," the priest answered, and with a bow he strode across the terrace to where Kalonay stood watching them.

II

Mrs. Carson and her daughter came from the hotel to the terrace through the hallway which divided the King's apartments. Baron Barrat preceded them and they followed in single file, Miss Carson walking first. It was a position her mother always forced upon her, and after people grew to know them they accepted it as illustrating Mrs. Carson's confidence in her daughter's ability to care for herself, as well as her own wish to remain in the background.

Patricia Carson, as she was named after her patron saint, or "Patty" Carson, as she was called more frequently, was an exceedingly pretty girl. She was tall and fair, with a smile that showed such confidence in everyone she met that few could find the courage to undeceive her by being themselves, and it was easier, in the face of such an appeal as her eyes made to the best in every one, for each to act a part while he was with her. She was young, impressionable, and absolutely inexperienced. As a little girl she had lived on a great ranch, where she could gallop from sunrise to sun-

35

set over her own prairie land, and later her life had been spent in a convent outside of Paris. She had but two great emotions, her love for her father and for the Church which had nursed her. Her father's death had sanctified him and given him a place in her heart that her mother could not hold, and when she found herself at twenty-one the mistress of a great fortune, her one idea as to the disposal of it was to do with it what would best please him and the Church which had been the ruling power in the life of both of them. She was quite unconscious of her beauty, and her mode of speaking was simple and eager.

She halted as she came near the King, and resting her two hands on the top of her lace parasol, nodded pleasantly to him and to the others. She neither courtesied nor offered him her hand, but seemed to prefer this middle course, leaving them to decide whether she acted as she did from ignorance or from choice.

As the King stepped forward to greet her mother, Miss Carson passed him and moved on to where the Father Superior stood apart from the others, talking earnestly with the Prince. What he was saying was of an unwelcome nature, for Kalonay's face wore an expression of boredom and polite protest which changed instantly to one of delight when he saw Miss Carson. The girl hesitated and made a deep obeisance to the priest.

"I am afraid I interrupt you," she said.

"Not at all," Kalonay assured her, laughing. "It is a most welcome interruption. The good father has been finding fault with me, as usual, and I am quite willing to change the subject."

The priest smiled kindly on the girl, and while he exchanged some words of welcome with her, Kalonay brought up one of the huge wicker chairs, and she seated herself with her back to the others, facing the two men, who stood leaning against the broad balustrade. They had been fellow-conspirators sufficiently long for them to have grown to know each other well, and the priest, so far from regarding her as an intruder, hailed her at once as a probable ally, and endeavored to begin again where he had ceased speaking.

"Do you not agree with me, Miss Carson?" he asked. "I am telling the Prince that zeal is not enough, and that high ideals, unless they are accompanied by good conduct, are futile. I want him to change, to be more sober, more strict——"

"Oh, you must not ask me," Miss Carson said, hurriedly, smiling and shaking her head. "We are working for only one thing, are we not? Beyond that you know nothing of me, and I know nothing of you. I came to hear of your visit," she continued; "am I to be told anything?" she asked, eagerly, looking from one to the other. "It has been such an anxious two weeks. We imagined all manner of things had happened to you."

Kalonay laughed happily. "The Father was probably never safer in his life," he said. "They took us to their hearts like brothers. They might have suffocated us with kindness, but we were in no other danger."

"Then you are encouraged, Father?" she asked, turning to the priest. "You found them loyal? Your visit was all you hoped, you can depend upon them?"

"We can count upon them absolutely," the monk assured her. "We shall start on our return voyage at once, in a day, as soon as his Majesty gives the word."

"There are so many things I want to know," the girl said; "but I have no right to ask," she added, looking up at him doubtfully.

"You have every right," the monk answered. "You have certainly earned it. Without the help you gave us we could not have moved. You have been more than generous——"

Miss Carson interrupted him with an impatient lifting of her head. "That sort of generosity is

nothing," she said. "With you men it is different.
You are all risking something. You are actually
helping, while I must sit still and wait. I hope,
Father," she said, smiling, "it is not wrong for me
to wish I were a man."

"Wrong!" exclaimed Kalonay, in a tone of
mock dismay; "of course it's wrong. It's wicked."

The monk turned and looked coldly over his
shoulder at Kalonay, and the Prince laughed.

"I beg your pardon," he said, "but we are told
to be contented with our lot," he argued, impeni-
tently. " 'He only is a slave who complains,' and
that is true even if a heretic did say it."

The monk shook his head and turned again to
Miss Carson with a tolerant smile.

"He is very young," he said, as though Kalonay
did not hear him, "and wild and foolish—and
yet," he added, doubtfully, "I find I love the boy."
He regarded the young man with a kind but im-
personal scrutiny, as though he were a picture or
a statue. "Sometimes I imagine he is all I might
have been," he said, "had not God given me the
strength to overcome myself. He has never de-
nied himself in anything; he is as wilful and capri-
cious as a girl. He makes a noble friend, Miss
Carson, and a generous enemy; but he is spoiled
irretrievably by good fortune and good living and

good health." The priest looked at the young man with a certain sad severity. " 'Unstable as water, thou shalt not excel,' " he said.

The girl, in great embarrassment, turned her head away, glancing from the ocean to the sky; but Kalonay seated himself coolly on the broad balustrade of the terrace with his hands on his hips, and his heels resting on the marble tiling, and clicked the soles of his boots together.

"Oh, I have had my bad days, too, Father," he said. He turned his head on one side, and pressed his lips together, looking down.

"Unstable as water—that is quite possible," he said, with an air of consideration; "but spoiled by good fortune—oh, no, that is not fair. Do you call it good fortune, sir," he laughed, "to be an exile at twenty-eight? Is it good fortune to be too poor to pay your debts, and too lazy to work; to be the last of a great name, and to have no chance to add to the glory of it, and no means to keep its dignity fresh and secure? Do you fancy I like to see myself drifting farther and farther away from the old standards and the old traditions; to have English brewers and German Jew bankers taking the place I should have, buying titles with their earnings and snubbing me because I can only hunt when someone gives me a mount, and because I choose to take a purse instead of a cup when we shoot at Monte Carlo?"

"What child's talk is this?" interrupted the priest, angrily. "A thousand horses cannot make a man noble, nor was poverty ever ignoble. You talk like a weak boy. Every word you say is your own condemnation. Why should you complain? Your bed is of your own making. The other prodigal was forced to herd with the swine—you have chosen to herd with them."

The girl straightened herself and half rose from her chair.

"You are boring Miss Carson with my delinquencies," said the Prince, sternly. His face was flushed, and he did not look either at the girl or at the priest.

"But the prodigal's father?" said Miss Carson, smiling at the older man. "Did he stand over him and upbraid him? You remember, he went to meet him when he was yet a great way off. That was it, was it not, Father?"

"Of course he did," cried Kalonay, laughing like a boy, and slipping lightly to the terrace. "He met him half way and gave him the best he had." He stepped to Miss Carson's side and the two young people moved away smiling, and the priest, seeing that they were about to escape him, cried eagerly, "But that prodigal had repented. This one——"

"Let's run," cried the Prince. "He will get the best of us if we stay. He always gets the best of me. He has been abusing me that way for two weeks now, and he is always sorry afterward. Let us leave him alone to his sorrow and remorse."

Kalonay walked across the terrace with Miss Carson, bending above her with what would have seemed to an outsider almost a proprietary right. She did not appear to notice it, but looked at him frankly and listened to what he had to say with interest. He was speaking rapidly, and as he spoke he glanced shyly at her as though seeking her approbation, and not boldly, as he was accustomed to do when he talked with either men or women. To look at her with admiration was such a cheap form of appreciation, and one so distasteful to her, that had he known it, Kalonay's averted eyes were more of a compliment than any words he could have spoken. His companions who had seen him with other women knew that his manner to her was not his usual manner, and that he gave her something he did not give to the others; that he was more discreet and less ready, and less at ease.

The Prince Kalonay had first met Miss Carson

and her mother by chance in Paris, at the rooms
of Father Paul, where they had each gone on the
same errand, and since that meeting his whole
manner toward the two worlds in which he lived
had altered so strangely that mere acquaintances
noticed the change.

Before he had met her, the little the priest had
said concerning her and her zeal for their common
desire had piqued his curiosity, and his imagination
had been aroused by the picture of a romantic
young woman giving her fortune to save the souls
of the people of Messina; his people whom he regarded and who regarded him less as a feudal lord
than as a father and a comrade. He had pictured
her as a nervous, angular woman with a pale,
ascetic face, and with the restless eyes of an enthu-
siast, dressed in black and badly dressed, and with
a severe and narrow intelligence. But he had prepared himself to forgive her personality, for the
sake of the high and generous impulse that inspired her. And when he was presented to her as
she really was, and found her young, lovable, and
nobly fair, the shock of wonder and delight had
held him silent during the whole course of her interview with the priest, and when she had left
them his brain was in a tumult and was filled with
memories of her words and gestures, and of the

sweet fearlessness of her manner. Beautiful women he had known before as beautiful women, but the saving grace in his nature had never before been so deeply roused by what was fine as well as beautiful. It seemed as though it were too complete and perfect. For he assured himself that she possessed everything—those qualities which he had never valued before because he believed them to be unattainable, and those others which he had made his idols. She was with him, mind and heart and soul, in the one desire of his life that he took seriously; she was of his religion, she was more noble than his noble sisters, and she was more beautiful than the day. In the first glow of the meeting it seemed to him as though fate had called them to do this work together,—she from the far shore of the Pacific, and he from his rocky island in the Middle Sea. And he saw with cruel distinctness, that if there were one thing wanting, it was himself. He worshipped her before he had bowed his first good-by to her, and that night he walked for miles up and down the long lengths of the avenue of the Champs-Élysées, facing the great change that she had brought into his life, but knowing himself to be utterly unfit for her coming. He felt like an unworthy steward caught at his master's return unprepared, with ungirt loins, and unlighted lamp. Nothing he had done since he was a child gave him the right to consider himself her equal. He was not blinded by the approaches which other daughters and the mothers of daughters had made him. He knew that what was enough to excuse many things in their eyes might find no apology in hers. He looked back with the awakening of a child at the irrevocable acts in his life that could not be altered nor dug up nor hidden away. They marked the road he had trodden like heavy milestones, telling his story to every passer-by. She could read them, as everyone else could read them. He had wasted his substance, he had bartered his birthright for a moment's pleasure; there was no one so low and despicable who could not call him comrade, to whom he had not given himself without reserve. There was nothing left, and now the one thing he had ever wanted had come, and had found him like a bankrupt, his credit wasted and his coffers empty. He had placed himself at the beck and call of every idle man and woman in Paris, and he was as common as the great clock-face that hangs above the boulevards.

Miss Carson's feelings toward Kalonay were not of her own choosing, and had passed through several stages. When they had first met she had thought it most sad that so careless and unprincipled a person should chance to hold so important a part in the task she had set herself to do. She knew his class only by hearsay, but she placed him in it, and, accordingly, at once dismissed him as a person from her mind. Kalonay had never shown her that he loved her, except by those signs which any woman can read and which no man can conceal; but he did not make love to her, and it was that which first prepossessed her in his favor. One or two other men who knew of her fortune, and to whom she had given as little encouragement as she had to Kalonay, had been less considerate. But his attitude toward her was always that of a fellow-worker in the common cause. He treated her with a gratitude for the help she meant to give his people which much embarrassed her. His seriousness pleased her with him, seeing, as she did, that it was not his nature to be serious, and his enthusiasm and love for his half-civilized countrymen increased her interest in them, and her liking for him. She could not help but admire the way in which he accepted, without forcing her to make it any plainer, the fact that he held no place in her thoughts. And then she found that he began to hold more of a place in her thoughts than she had supposed any man could hold of whom she

knew so little, and of whom the little she knew
was so ill. She missed him when she went to the
priest's and found that he had not sent for Kalonay to bear his part in their councils; and at times
she felt an unworthy wish to hear Kalonay speak
the very words she had admired him for keeping
from her. And at last she learned the truth that
she did love him, and it frightened her, and made
her miserable and happy. They had not seen each
other since he had left Paris for Messina, and
though they spoke now only of his mission to the
island, there was back of what they said the joy
for each of them of being together again and of
finding that it meant so much. What it might
mean to the other, neither knew.

For some little time the King followed the two
young people with his eyes, and then joined them,
making signs to Kalonay that he wished him to
leave them together; but Kalonay remained blind
to his signals, and Barrat, seeing that it was not a
tête-à-tête, joined them also. When he did so
Kalonay asked the King for a word, and laying
his hand upon his arm walked with him down the
terrace, pointing ostensibly to where the yacht lay
in the harbor. Louis answered his pantomime
with an appropriate gesture, and then asked,
sharply, "Well, what is it? Why did you bring

me here? And what do you mean by staying on when you see you are not wanted?"

They were some distance from the others. Kalonay smiled and made a slight bow. "Your Majesty," he began, with polite emphasis. The King looked at him curiously.

"In the old days under similar circumstances," the Prince continued, with the air of a courtier rather than that of an equal, "had I thought of forming an alliance by marriage, I should have come to your Majesty first and asked your gracious approval. But those days are past, and we are living at the end of the century; and we do such things differently." He straightened himself and returned the King's look of amused interest with one as cynical as his own. "What I wanted to tell you, Louis," he said, quietly, "is that I mean to ask Miss Carson to become the Princess Kalonay."

The King raised his head quickly and stared at the younger man with a look of distaste and surprise. He gave an incredulous laugh.

"Indeed?" he said at last. "There was always something about rich women you could never resist."

The Prince made his acknowledgment with a shrug of his shoulders and smiled indifferently.

"I didn't expect you to understand," he said. "It does seem odd; it's quite as difficult for me to understand as for you. I have been through it a great many times, and I thought I knew all there was of it. But now it seems different. No, it does not seem different," he corrected himself; "it is different, and I love the lady and I mean to ask her to do me the honor to marry me. I didn't expect you to understand, I don't care if you do. I only wanted to warn you."

"Warn me?" interrupted the King, with an unpleasant smile. "Indeed! against what? Your tone is a trifle peremptory—but you are interesting, most interesting! Kalonay in a new rôle, Kalonay in love! Most interesting! Warn me against what?" he repeated sharply.

"Your Majesty has a certain manner," the Prince began, with a pretence of hesitation, "a charm of manner, I might say, which is proverbial. It is, we know, attractive to women. Every woman acknowledges it. But your Majesty is sometimes too gracious. He permits himself to condescend to many women, to any woman, to women of all classes——"

"That will do," said the King; "what do you mean?"

"What I mean is this," said Kalonay, lowering

his voice and looking into the King's half-closed
eyes. "You can have all of Miss Carson's money
you want—all you can get. I don't want it. If I
am to marry her at all, I am not marrying her for
her money. You can't believe that. It isn't essen-
tial that you should. But I want you to leave the
woman I hope to make my wife alone. I will
allow no pretty speeches, nor royal attentions.
She can give her money where she pleases, now
and always; but I'll not have her eyes opened to—
as you can open them. I will not have her annoyed. And if she is——"

"Ah, and if she is?" challenged the King. His
eyes were wide apart now and his lips were parted
and drawn back from his teeth, like a snarling
cat——

"I shall hold whoever annoys her responsible,"
Kalonay concluded, impersonally.

There was a moment's pause, during which the
two men stood regarding each other warily.

Then the King stiffened his shoulders and placed
his hands slowly behind his back. "That sounds,
my dear Kalonay," he said, "almost like a
threat."

The younger man laughed insolently. "I meant
it, too, your Majesty," he answered, bowing mockingly and backing away.

The King's Jackal

As the King's guests seated themselves at his breakfast-table Louis smiled upon them with a gracious glance of welcome and approval. His manner was charmingly condescending, and in his appearance there was nothing more serious than an anxiety for their better entertainment and a certain animal satisfaction in the food upon his plate.

In reality his eyes were distributing the people at the table before him into elements favorable or unfavorable to his plans, and in his mind he shuffled them and their values for him or against him as a gambler arranges and rearranges the cards in his hand. He saw himself plainly as his own highest card, and Barrat and Erhaupt as willing but mediocre accomplices. In Father Paul and Kalonay he recognized his most powerful allies or most dangerous foes. Miss Carson meant nothing to him but a source from which he could draw the sinews of war. What would become of her after the farce was ended, he did not consider. He was not capable of comprehending either her or her motives, and had he concerned himself about her at all, he would have probably thought that she was more of a fool than the saint she pretended to be, and that she had come to their assistance more because she wished to be near a Prince and a King than because she cared for the souls of sixty thousand peasants. That she would surely lose her money, and could hardly hope to escape from them without losing her good name, did not concern him. It was not his duty to look after the reputation of any American heiress who thought she could afford to be unconventional. She had a mother to do that for her, and she was pretty enough, he concluded, to excuse many things,— so pretty that he wondered if he might brave the Countess Zara and offer Miss Carson the attentions to which Kalonay had made such arrogant objections. The King smiled at the thought, and let his little eyes fall for a moment on the tall figure of the girl with its crown of heavy golden hair, and on her clever, earnest eyes. She was certainly worth waiting for, and in the meanwhile she was virtually unprotected and surrounded by his own people. According to his translation of her acts, she had already offered him every encouragement, and had placed herself in a position which to his understanding of the world could have but one interpretation. What Kalonay's sudden infatuation might mean he could not foresee; whether it promised good or threatened evil, he could only guess, but he decided that the young man's unwonted show of independence of the morning must be punished. His claim to exclu-

"He Will Get the Best of Us if We Stay."

sive proprietorship in the young girl struck the
King as amusing, but impertinent. It would be
easy sailing in spite of all, he decided; for somewhere up above them in the hotel sat the unbidden
guest, the woman against whom Father Paul had
raised the ban of expulsion, but who had, nevertheless, tricked both him and the faithful Jackal.

The breakfast was drawing to an end and the
faithful Niccolas was the only servant remaining
in the room. The talk had grown intimate and
touched openly upon the successful visit of the two
ambassadors to the island, and of Barrat's mission to Paris. Of Madame Zara's visit to the
northern half of the island, which was supposed to
have been less successful, no mention was made.

Louis felt as he listened to them like a man at
a play, who knows that at a word from him the
complications would cease, and that were he to
rise in the stalls and explain them away, and point
out the real hero and denounce the villain, the cur-
tain would have to ring down on the instant. He
gave a little purr of satisfaction, and again mar-
shalled his chances before him and smiled to find
them good. He was grandly at peace with himself and with the world. Whatever happened, he
was already richer by some 300,000 francs, and
in a day, if he could keep the American girl to her

promise, would be as rich again. When the farce
of landing his expedition had been played he
would be free,—free to return to his clubs and to
his boulevards and boudoirs, with money enough
to silence the most insolent among his creditors,
and with renewed credit; with even a certain
glamour about him of one who had dared to do,
even though he had failed in the doing, who had
shaken off the slothfulness of ease and had chosen
to risk his life for his throne with a smoking rifle
in his hand, until a traitor had turned fortune
against him.

The King was amused to find that this prospect
pleased him vastly. He was surprised to discover
that, careless as he thought himself to be to public
opinion, he was still capable of caring for its approbation; but he consoled himself for this weakness
by arguing that it was only because the approbation would be his by a trick that it pleased him to
think of. Perhaps some of his royal cousins, in
the light of his bold intent, might take him under
their protection instead of neglecting him shame-
fully, as they had done in the past. His armed
expedition might open certain doors to him; his
name—and he smiled grimly as he imagined it—
would ring throughout Europe as the Soldier
King, as the modern disciple of the divine right of

kings. He saw, in his mind's eye, even the possibility of a royal alliance and a pension from one of the great Powers. No matter where he looked he could see nothing but gain to himself, more power for pleasure, more chances of greater fortune in the future, and while his lips assented to what the others said, and his eyes thanked them for some expression of loyalty or confidence, he saw himself in dreams as bright as an absinthe drinker's, back in his beloved Paris: in the Champs-Élysées behind fine horses, lolling from a silk box at the opera, dealing baccarat at the Jockey Club, or playing host to some beautiful woman of the hour, in the new home he would establish for her in the discreet and leafy borders of the Bois.

He had forgotten his guests and the moment. He had forgotten that there were difficulties yet to overcome, and with a short, indrawn sigh of pleasure, he threw back his head and smiled arrogantly upon the sunny terrace and the green palms and the brilliant blue sea, as though he challenged the whole beautiful world before him to do aught but minister to his success and contribute to his pleasures.

And at once, as though in answer to his challenge, a tall, slim young man sprang lightly up the steps of the terrace, passed the bewildered guards with a cheery nod, and, striding before the open windows, knocked with his fist upon the portals of the door, as sharply and as confidently as though the King's shield had hung there, and he had struck it with a lance.

The King's dream shattered and faded away at the sound, and he moved uneasily in his chair. He had the gambler's superstitious regard for trifles, and this invasion of his privacy by a confident stranger filled him with sudden disquiet.

He saw Kalonay staring at the open windows with an expression of astonishment and dismay.

"Who is it?" the King asked, peevishly. "What are you staring at? How did he get in?"

Kalonay turned on Barrat, sitting at his right. "Did you see him?" he asked. Barrat nodded gloomily.

"The devil!" exclaimed the Prince, as though Barrat had confirmed his guess. "I beg your pardon," he said, nodding his head toward the women. He pushed back his chair and stood irresolutely with his napkin in his hand. "Tell him we are not in, Niccolas," he commanded.

"He saw us as he passed the window," the Baron objected.

"Say we are at breakfast then. I will see him

myself in a moment. What shall I tell him?" he asked, turning to Barrat. "Do you think he knows? He must know, they have told him in Paris."

"You are keeping us waiting," said the King. "What is it? Who is this man?"

"An American named Gordon. He is a correspondent," Kalonay answered, without turning his head. His eyes were still fixed on the terrace as though he had seen a ghost.

The King slapped his hand on the arm of the chair. "You promised me," he said, "that we should be free from that sort of thing. That is why I agreed to come here instead of going to Algiers. Go out, Barrat, and send him away."

Barrat pressed his lips together and shook his head.

"You can't send him away like that," he said. "He is a very important young man."

"Find out how much he will take, then," exclaimed the King, angrily, "and give it to him. I can better afford to pay blackmail to any amount than have my plans spoiled now by the newspapers. Give him what he wants—a fur coat—they always wear fur coats—or five thousand francs, or something—anything—but get rid of him."

Barrat stirred uneasily in his chair and shrugged

his shoulders. "He is not a boulevard journalist," he replied, sulkily.

"Your Majesty is thinking of the Hungarian Jews at Vienna," explained Kalonay, "who live on *chantage* and the Monte Carlo propaganda fund. This man is not in their class; he is not to be bought. I said he was an American."

"An American!" exclaimed Mrs. Carson and her daughter, exchanging rapid glances. "Is it Archie Gordon you mean?" the girl asked. "I thought he was in China."

"That is the man—Archie Gordon. He writes books and explores places," Kalonay answered.

"I know him. He wrote a book on the slave trade in the Congo," contributed Colonel Erhaupt. "I met him at Zanzibar. What does he want with us?"

"He was in Yokohama when the Japanese-Chinese war broke out," said Kalonay, turning to the King, "and he cabled a London paper he would follow the war for it if they paid him a hundred a week. He meant American dollars, but they thought he meant pounds, so they cabled back that they'd pay one-half that sum. He answered, 'One hundred or nothing,' and they finally assented to that, and he started; and when the first week's remittance arrived, and he received five hundred dollars instead of the one hundred he expected, he sent back the difference."

"What a remarkable young man!" exclaimed the King. "He is much too good for daily wear. We don't want anyone like that around here, do we?"

"I know Mr. Gordon very well," said Miss Carson. "He lived in San Francisco before he came East. He was always at our house, and was a great friend of the family; wasn't he, mother? We haven't seen him for two years now, but I know he wouldn't spoil our plans for the sake of his paper, if he knew we were in earnest, if he understood that everything depended upon its being kept a secret."

"We are not certain that he knows anything," the King urged. "He may not have come here to see us. I think Father Paul should talk with him first."

"I was going to suggest," said Miss Carson, with some hesitation, "that if I spoke to him I might be able to put it to him in such a way that he would see how necessary it——"

"Oh, excellent!" exclaimed the King, eagerly, and rising to his feet; "if you only would be so kind, Miss Carson."

Kalonay, misunderstanding the situation altogether, fastened his eyes upon the table and did not speak.

"He has not come to see you, Patricia," said Mrs. Carson, quietly.

"He does not know that I am here," Miss Carson answered; "but I'm sure if he did he would be very glad to see us again. And if we do see him we can make him promise not to do anything that might interfere with our plans. Won't you let me speak to him, mother?"

Mrs. Carson turned uncertainly to the priest for direction, and his glance apparently reassured her, for she rose, though still with a troubled countenance, and the two women left the room together, the men standing regarding each other anxiously across the table. When they had gone the King lit a cigarette and, turning his back on his companions, puffed at it nervously in silence. Kalonay sat moodily studying the pattern on the plate before him, and the others whispered together at the farther end of the table.

When Miss Carson and her mother stepped out upon the terrace, the American was standing with his back toward them and was speaking to the guards who sat cross-legged at the top of the steps. They showed no sign of surprise at the fact of his addressing them in their own tongue further than that they answered him with a show of respect which they had not exhibited toward those they protected. The American turned as he heard the footsteps behind him, and, after a startled look of astonishment, hurried toward the two women, exclaiming, with every expression of pleasure.

"I had no idea you were stopping here," he said, after the first greetings were over. "I thought you were somewhere on the Continent. I am so glad I caught you. It seems centuries since I saw you last. You're looking very well, Mrs. Carson— and as for Patty—I am almost afraid of her—I've been hearing all sorts of things about you lately, Patty," he went on, turning a smiling countenance toward the girl. "About your engagements to princes and dukes—all sorts of disturbing rumors. What a terrible swell you've grown to be. I hardly recognize you at all, Mrs. Carson. It isn't possible this is the same young girl I used to take buggy riding on Sunday evenings?"

"Indeed, it is not. I wish it were," said Mrs. Carson, plaintively, sinking into a chair. "I'm glad to see you're not changed, Archie," she added, with a sigh.

"Why, he's very much changed, mother," the girl said. "He's taller, and, in comparison with what he was, he's almost wasted away, and so sun-

The King's Jackal

burned I hardly knew him. Except round the forehead," she added, mockingly, "and I suppose the sun couldn't burn there because of the laurel-wreaths. I hear they bring them to you fresh every morning."

"They're better than coronets, at any rate," Gordon answered, with a nod. "They're not so common. And if I'm wasted away, can you wonder? How long has it been since I saw you, Patty?"

"No, I'm wrong, he's not changed," Miss Carson said dryly, as she seated herself beside her mother.

"How do you two come to be stopping here?" the young man asked. "I thought this hotel had been turned over to King Louis?"

"It has," Mrs. Carson answered. "We are staying at the Continental, on the hill there. We are only here for breakfast. He asked us to breakfast."

"He?" repeated Gordon, with an incredulous smile. "Who? Not the King—not that blackguard?"

Miss Carson raised her head, and stared at him in silence, and her mother gave a little gasp, apparently of relief and satisfaction.

"Yes," Miss Carson answered at last, coldly.

The King's Jackal

"We are breakfasting with him. What do you know against him?"

Gordon stared at her with such genuine astonishment that the girl lowered her eyes, and, bending forward in her chair, twirled her parasol nervously between her fingers.

"What do I know against him? Why, Patty!" he exclaimed. "How did you meet him, in Heaven's name?" he asked, roughly. "Have you been seen with him? Have you known him long? Who had the impudence to present him?"

Mrs. Carson looked up, now thoroughly alarmed. Her lower lip was trembling, and she twisted her gloved hands together in her lap.

"What do you know against him?" Miss Carson repeated, meeting Gordon's look with one as full of surprise as his own.

The young man regarded her steadily for a few moments, and then, with a change of manner, as though he now saw the situation was much more serious than he had at first supposed, drew up a chair in front of the two women and seated himself deliberately.

"Has he borrowed any money from you yet?" he asked. Miss Carson's face flushed crimson and she straightened her shoulders and turned her eyes away from Gordon with every sign of indignation and disapproval. The young man gave an exclamation of relief.

"No? That's good. You cannot have known him so very long. I am greatly relieved."

"Louis of Messina," he began more gently, "is the most unscrupulous rascal in Europe. Since they turned him out of his kingdom he has lived by selling his title to men who are promoting new brands of champagne or floating queer mining shares. The greater part of his income is dependent on the generosity of the old nobility of Messina, and when they don't pay him readily enough, he levies blackmail on them. He owes money to every tailor and horse-dealer and hotel-keeper in Europe, and no one who can tell one card from another will play with him. That is his reputation. And to help him live up to it he has surrounded himself with a parcel of adventurers as rascally as himself: a Colonel Erhaupt who was dropped from a German regiment, and who is a Colonel only by the favor of the Queen of Madagascar; a retired croupier named Barrat; and a fallen angel called Kalonay, a fellow of the very best blood in Europe and with the very worst morals. They call him the King's Jackal, and he is one of the most delightful blackguards I ever met. So is the King for that matter, a most entertaining individual if you keep him in his place, but a man no woman can know. In fact, Mrs. Carson," Gordon went on, addressing himself to the mother, "when you have to say that a woman has absolutely no reputation whatever you can best express it by explaining that she has a title from Louis of Messina. That is his Majesty's way of treating his feminine friends when they bore him and he wants to get rid of them. He gives them a title.

"The only thing the man ever did that was to his credit and that could be discussed in polite society is what he is doing now at this place, at this moment. For it seems," Gordon whispered, drawing his chair closer, "that he is about to show himself something of a man after all, and that he is engaged in fitting out an armed expedition with which he hopes to recover his kingdom. That's what brought me here, and I must say I rather admire him for attempting such a thing. Of course, it was Kalonay who put him up to it; he would never have stirred from the boulevards if that young man had not made him. But he is here, nevertheless, waiting for a favorable opportunity to sail, and he has ten thousand rifles and three Maxim guns lying in his yacht out there in the harbor. That's how I came to learn about it. I was getting an estimate on an outfit I was thinking of taking into Yucatan from my old gunsmith in the Rue Scribe, and he dropped a hint that he had shipped ten thousand rifles to Tangier, to Colonel Erhaupt. I have met Erhaupt in Zanzibar, and knew he was the King's right-hand man, so I put two and two together and decided I would follow them up, and——"

"Yes, and now," interrupted Miss Carson, sharply—"and now that you have followed them up, what do you mean to do?"

Gordon looked his surprise at her earnestness, but answered that he did not know what he would do; he thought he would either ask them to give him a commission in their expedition, and let him help them fight, and write an account of their adventures later, or he would telegraph the story at once to his paper. It was with him, he said, entirely a question as to which course would be of the greater news value. If he told what he now knew, his paper would be the first of all others to inform the world of the expedition and the proposed revolution; while if he volunteered for the expedition and waited until it had failed or succeeded, he would be able to tell more eventually, but would have to share it with other correspondents.

The King's Jackal

Miss Carson regarded him with an expression in which indignation and entreaty were curiously blended.

"Archie," she said, in a low voice, "you do not know what you are doing or saying. You are threatening to spoil the one thing in my life on which I have set my heart. The return of this man to his throne, whether he is worthy or not, means the restoration of the Catholic Church on that island; it means the return of the monks and the rebuilding of the monasteries, and the salvation of sixty thousand souls. I know all that they mean to do. I am the one who paid for those rifles that brought you here; you have told me only what I have known for months, and for which I have been earnestly working and praying. I am not blinded by these men. They are not the creatures you describe; but no matter what they may be, it is only through them, and through them alone, that I can do what I have set out to do."

Gordon silenced her with a sweep of his hand.

"Do you mean to tell me," he demanded, "that you are mixed up in this—with these—that they have taken money from you, and told you they meant to use it to re-establish the Church? Mrs. Carson," he exclaimed, bitterly, turning upon her, "why have you allowed this—what have you been

67

doing while this was going on? Do you suppose those scoundrels care for the Church—the Church, indeed! Wait until I see them—any of them—Erhaupt by choice, and I'll make them give up every franc you've lent them, or I'll horsewhip and expose them for the gang of welshers and thimble-riggers they are; or if they prefer their own methods, I'll call them out in rotation and shoot their arms and legs off." He stopped and drew a long breath, either of content that he had discovered the situation in time to take some part in it, or at the prospect of a fight.

"The idea of you two helpless females wandering into this den of wolves!" he exclaimed, indignantly. "It's about time you had a man to look after you! You go back to your hotel now, and let me have a chat with Louis of Messina. He's. kept me waiting some twenty minutes as it is, and that's a little longer than I can give him. I'm not a creditor." He rose from his chair; but Miss Carson put out her hand and motioned him to be seated.

"Archie," she said, "I like the way you take this, even though you are all wrong about it, because it's just like you to fly into a passion and want to fight someone for somebody. If your conclusions were anywhere near the truth, you would

be acting very well. But they are not. The King
is not handling my money, nor the Prince Kalonay.
It is in the keeping of Father Paul, the Father
Superior of the Dominican monks, who is the only
one of these people I know or who knows me. He
is not a swindler, too, is he, or a retired croupier?
Listen to me now, and do not fly out like that at
me, or at mother. It is not her fault. Last summer mother and I went to Messina as tourists, and
one day, when passing through a seaport town, we
saw a crowd of people on the shore, standing or
kneeling by the hundreds in a great semicircle close
to the water's edge. There was a priest preaching
to them from an open boat. It was like a scene
from the New Testament, and the man, this Father
Paul, made me think of one of the disciples. I
asked them why he did not preach on the land, and
they told me that he and all of the priests had been
banished from the island six years before, and that
they could only return by stealth and dared not
land except by night. When the priest had finished speaking, I had myself rowed out to his boat,
and I talked a long time with him, and he told me
of this plan to re-establish himself and his order.
I offered to help him with my money, and he promised me a letter to Cardinal Napoli. It reached
me on my return to Rome, and through the influ-

ence of the Cardinal I was given an audience with
the Pope, and I was encouraged to aid Father Paul
as far as I could. I had meant to build a memorial
church for father, but they urged me to give the
money instead to this cause. All my dealings until
to-day have been with Father Paul alone. I have
seen a little of the Prince Kalonay because they
are always together; but he has always treated me
in a way to which no one could take exception, and
he is certainly very much in earnest. When Father
Paul left Paris mother and I came on here in order
to be near him, and that is how you find me at
Tangier. And now that you understand how
much this means to me, I know you will not do
anything to stand in our way. Those men inside
are afraid that you came here for just the reason
that apparently has brought you, and when they
saw you a little while ago through the windows
they were greatly disturbed. Let me tell them
that you mean to volunteer for the campaign. The
King cannot refuse the services of a man who has
done the things you are always doing. And I
promise you that for a reward you shall be the
only one to tell the story of our attempt. I promise you," she repeated earnestly, "that the day we
enter the capital, you can cable whatever you please
and tell our story to the whole of Europe."

"The story be hanged!" replied Gordon. "You have made this a much more serious business than a newspaper story. You misunderstand me utterly, Patty. I am here now because I am not going to have you compromised and robbed."

The girl stood up and looked down at the young man indignantly.

"You have no right whatever to use that tone to me," she said. "I am of age and my own adviser. I am acting for the good of a great number of people, and according to what my conscience and common sense tell me is right. I shall hate you if you attempt to interfere. You can do one of two things, Archie. I give you your choice: you can either go with them as a volunteer, and promise to keep our secret; or you can cable what you know now, what you know only by accident, but if you do, you will lose your best friend, and you will defeat a good and a noble effort."

Gordon leaned back in his chair, and looked up at her steadily for a brief moment, and then rose with a smile, and bowed to the two women in silence. He crossed the terrace quickly with an amused and puzzled countenance, and walked into the breakfast-room, from the windows of which, as he rightly guessed, the five conspirators had for some time observed him. He looked from one to the other of the men about the table, until his eyes finally met those of the King.

"I believe, sir, you are leading an expedition against the Republic of Messina?" Gordon said. "I am afraid it can't start unless you take me with you."

III

The presence in Tangier of the King of Messina and his suite, and the arrival there of the French noblemen who had volunteered for the expedition, could not escape the observation of the resident Consuls-General and of the foreign colony, and dinners, riding and hunting parties, pig-sticking, and excursions on horseback into the outlying country were planned for their honor and daily entertainment. Had the conspirators held aloof from these, the residents might have asked, since it was not to enjoy themselves, what was the purpose of their stay in Tangier; and so, to allay suspicion as to their real object, different members of the expedition had been assigned from time to time to represent the visitors at these festivities. On the morning following the return of the yacht from Messina, an invitation to ride to a farmhouse some miles out of Tangier and to breakfast there had been sent to the visitors, and the King had directed the Prince Kalonay, and half of the delegation from Paris, to accept it in his name.

The King's Jackal

They were well content to go, and rode forth gayly and in high spirits, for the word had been brought them early in the morning that the expedition was already prepared to move, and that same evening at midnight the yacht would set sail for Messina. They were careless as to what fortune waited for them there. The promise of much excitement, of fighting and of danger, of possible honor and success, stirred the hearts of the young men gloriously, and as they galloped across the plains, or raced each other from point to point, or halted to jump their ponies across the many gaping crevices which the sun had split in the surface of the plain, they filled the still, warm air with their shouts and laughter. In the party there were many ladies, and the groups changed and formed again as they rode forward, spread out on either side of the caravan-trail and covering the plain like a skirmish line of cavalry. But Kalonay kept close at Miss Carson's stirrup, whether she walked her pony or sent him flying across the hard, sunbaked soil.

"I hope you won't do that again," he said, earnestly, as she drew up panting, with her sailor hat and hair falling to her shoulders. They had been galloping recklessly over the open crevices in the soil.

74

The King's Jackal

"It's quite the nastiest country I ever saw," he said. "It looks as though an earthquake had shaken it open and had forgotten to close it again. Believe me, it is most unsafe and dangerous. Your pony might stumble—" He stopped, as though the possibilities were too serious for words, but the girl laughed.

"It's no more dangerous than riding across our prairie at dusk when you can't see the barbed wire. You are the last person in the world to find fault because a thing is dangerous," she added.

They had reached the farm, where they went to breakfast, and the young Englishman who was their host was receiving his guests in his garden, and the servants were passing among them, carrying cool drinks and powdered sweets and Turkish coffee. Kalonay gave their ponies to a servant and pointed with his whip to an arbor that stood at one end of the garden.

"May we sit down there a moment until they call us?" he said. "I have news of much importance—and I may not have another chance," he begged, looking at her wistfully. The girl stood motionless; her eyes were serious, and she measured the distance down the walk to the arbor as though she saw it beset with dangers more actual than precipices and twisted wire. The Prince

75

watched her as though his fate was being weighed
in his presence.

"Very well," she said at last, and moved on
before him down the garden-path.

The arbor was open to the air with a low, broad
roof of palm-leaves that overhung it on all sides
and left it in deep shadow. Around it were many
strange plants and flowers, some native to Morocco
and some transplanted from their English home.
From where they sat they could see the other
guests moving in and out among the groves of
orange and olive trees and swaying palms, and
standing, outlined against the blue sky, upon the
low, flat roof of the farm-house.

"I have dared to ask you to be so good as to
give me this moment," the Prince said humbly,
"only because I am going away, and it may be my
last chance to speak with you. You do not mind?
You do not think I presume?"

"No, I do not mind," said the girl, smiling.
"In my country we do not think it a terrible of-
fence to talk to a girl at a garden-party. But you
said there was something of importance you
wanted to say to me. You mean the expedition?"

"Yes," said Kalonay. "We start this evening."

The girl raised her head slightly and stared past
him at the burning white walls and the burning

blue sky that lay outside the circle of shadow in which they sat.

"This evening—" she repeated to herself.

"We reach there in two days," Kalonay continued; "and then we—then we go on—until we enter the capital."

The girl's head was bent, and she looked at her hands as they lay in her lap and frowned at them, they seemed so white and pretty and useless.

"Yes, you go on," she repeated, "and we stay here. You are a man and able to go on. I know what that means. And you like it," she added, with a glance of mingled admiration and fear. "You are glad to fight and to risk death and to lead men on to kill other men."

Kalonay drew lines in the sand with his riding-whip, and did not raise his head.

"I suppose it is because you are fighting for your home," the girl continued, "and to set your country free, and that you can live with your own people again, and because it is a holy war. That must be it. Now that it is really come, I see it all differently. I see things I had not thought about before. They frighten me," she said.

The Prince raised his head and faced the girl, clasping the end of his whip nervously in his hand.

"If we should win the island for the King," he

said, "I believe it will make a great change in me.
I shall be able to go freely then to my home, as
you say, to live there always, to give up the life
I have led on the Continent. It has been a foolish
life—a dog's life—and I have no one to blame for
it but myself. I made it worse than it need to
have been. But if we win, I have promised myself
that I will not return to it; and if we fail I shall
not return to it, for the reason that I shall have
been killed. I shall have much power if we win.
When I say much power, I mean much power in
Messina, in that little corner of the world, and I
wish to use it worthily and well. I am afraid I
should not have thought of it," he went on,
naïvely, as though he were trying to be quite fair,
"had not Father Paul pointed out to me what I
should do, how I could raise the people and stop
the abuses which made them drive us from the
island. The people must be taxed less heavily,
and the money must be spent for them and not for
us, on roads and harbors and schools, not at the
Palace on banquets and fêtes. These are Father
Paul's ideas, not mine,—but now I make them
mine." He rose and paced the length of the little
arbor, his hands clasped behind him and his eyes
bent on the ground. "Yes, that is what I mean to
do," he said. "That is the way I mean to live.

"I Suppose it is because You are Fighting for your Home."

The King's Jackal

And if we fail, I mean to be among those who are to die on the fortifications of the capital, so that with me the Kalonay family will end, and end fighting for the King, as many of my people have done before me. There is no other way. For me there shall be no more idleness nor exile. I must either live on to help my people, or I must die with them." He stopped in his walk and regarded the girl closely. "You may be thinking, it is easy for him to promise this, it is easy to speak of what one will do. I know that. I know that I can point back at nothing I have done that gives me any right to ask you to believe me now. But I do ask it, for if you believe me—believe what I say—it makes it easier for me to tell you why after this I must live worthily. But you know why? You must know; it is not possible that you do not know."

He sat down beside her on the bench, leaning forward and crushing his hands together on his knee. "It is because I love you. Because I love you so that everything which is not worthy is hateful to me, myself most of all. It is the only thing that counts. I used to think I knew what love meant; I used to think love was a selfish thing that needed love in return, that it must be fed on love to live, that it needed vows and tender speeches

and caresses, or it would die. I know now that
when one truly cares, he does not ask whether the
other cares or not. It is what one gives that
counts, not what one receives. You have given me
nothing—nothing—not a word nor a look; yet
since I have known you I have been more madly
happy in just knowing that you live than I would
have been had any other woman in all the world
thrown herself into my arms and said she loved me
above all other men. I am not fit to tell you this.
But to-night I go to try myself, either never to see
you again, or to come back perhaps more worthy
to love you. Think of this when I am gone. Do
not speak to me now. I may have made you hate
me for speaking so, or I may have made you pity
me; so let me go not knowing, just loving you, wor-
shipping you, and holding you apart and above all
other people. I go to fight for you, do you understand? Not for our Church, not for my people,
but for you, to live or die for you. And I ask
nothing from you but that you will let me love
you always."

The Prince bent, and catching up Miss Carson's
riding-gloves that lay beside her on the bench,
kissed them again and again, and then, rising
quickly, walked out of the arbor into the white
sunshine, and, without turning, mounted his pony

and galloped across the burning desert in the direction of Tangier.

Archie Gordon had not been invited to join the excursion into the country, nor would he have accepted it, for he wished to be by himself that he might review the situation and consider what lay before him. He sat with his long legs dangling over the broad rampart which overlooks the harbor of Tangier. He was whistling meditatively to himself and beating an accompaniment to the tune with his heels. At intervals he ceased whistling while he placed a cigar between his teeth and pulled upon it thoughtfully, resuming his tune again at the point where it had been interrupted. Below him the waves ran up lazily on the level beach and sank again, dragging the long sea-weed with them, as they swept against the sharp rocks, and exposed them for an instant, naked and glistening in the sun. On either side of him the town stretched to meet the low, white, sand-hills in a crescent of low, white houses pierced by green minarets and royal palms. A warm sun had sent the world to sleep at mid-day, and an enforced peace hung over the glaring white town and the sparkling blue sea. Gordon blinked at the glare, but his eyes showed no signs of drowsiness. They

were, on the contrary, awake to all that passed on
the high road behind him, and on the sandy beach
at his feet, while at the same time his mind was
busily occupied in reviewing what had occurred the
day before, and in adjusting new conditions. At
the hotel he had found that the situation was becoming too complicated, and that it was impossible
to feel sure of the truth of anything, or of the
sincerity of anyone. Since the luncheon hour the
day before he had become a fellow-conspirator
with men who were as objectionable to him in
every way as he knew he was obnoxious to them.
But they had been forced to accept him because,
so they supposed, he had them at the mercy of his
own pleasure. He knew their secret, and in the
legitimate pursuit of his profession he could, if he
chose, inform the island of Messina, with the rest
of the world, of their intention toward it, and
bring their expedition to an end, though he had
chosen, as a reward for his silence, to become one
of themselves. Only the Countess Zara had
guessed the truth, that it was Gordon himself who
was at their mercy, and that so long as the American girl persisted in casting her fortunes with
them her old young friend was only too eager to
make any arrangement with them that would keep
him at her side.

The King's Jackal

It was a perplexing position, and Gordon turned it over and over in his mind. Had it not been that Miss Carson had a part in it he would have enjoyed the adventure, as an adventure, keenly. He had no objections to fighting on the side of rascals, or against rascals. He objected to them only in the calmer moments of private life; and as he was of course ignorant that the expedition was only a make-believe, he felt a certain respect for his fellow-conspirators as men who were willing to stake their lives for a chance of better fortune. But that their bravery was of the kind which would make them hesitate to rob and deceive a helpless girl he very much doubted; for he knew that even the bravest of warriors on their way to battle will requisition a herd of cattle or stop to loot a temple. The day before, Gordon had witnessed the brief ceremony which attended the presentation of the young noblemen from Paris who had volunteered for the expedition in all good faith, and he reviewed it and analyzed it as he sat smoking on the ramparts.

It had been an impressive ceremony, in spite of the fact that so few had taken part in it, but the earnestness of the visitors and the enthusiasm of Kalonay and the priest had made up for the lack of numbers. The scene had appealed to him as

one of the most dramatic he had witnessed in the
pursuit of a calling in which looking on at real
dramas was the most frequent duty, and he had enjoyed the strange mixture of ancient terms of ad-
dress and titles with the modern manners of the
men themselves. It had interested him to watch
Baron Barrat bring out the ancient crown and
jewelled sceptre which had been the regalia of all
the Kings of Messina since the Crusades and
spread them out upon a wicker tea-table, from
which Niccolas had just removed some empty
coffee-cups, half filled with the ends of cigarettes,
some yellow-backed novels, and a copy of the
Paris *Figaro*. It was also interesting to him to
note how the sight of the little heir-apparent af-
fected both the peasants from the mountains and
the young nobles from the Club Royale. The
former fell upon their knees with the tears rolling
down the furrows in their tanned cheeks, while the
little wise-eyed boy stood clinging to his nurse's
skirts with one hand and to his father's finger with
the other, and nodded his head at them gravely
like a toy mandarin.

Then the King had addressed them in a digni-
fied, earnest, and almost eloquent speech, and had
promised much and prophesied the best of fortunes, and then, at the last, had turned suddenly

toward Miss Carson, where she stood in the background between her mother and Father Paul.

"Every cause has its Joan of Arc, or its Maria Theresa," he cried, looking steadfastly at Miss Carson. "No cause has succeeded without some good woman to aid it. To help us, my friends, we have a daughter of the people, as was Joan of Arc, and a queen, as was Maria Theresa, for she comes from that country where every woman is a queen in her own right, and where the love of liberty is inherent." The King took a quick step backward, and taking Miss Carson's hand drew her forward beside him and placed her facing his audience, while the girl made vain efforts to withdraw her hand. "This is she," he said earnestly, "the true daughter of the Church who has made it possible for us to return to our own again. It is due to her that the King of Messina shall sit once more on his throne; it is through her generosity alone that the churches will rise from their ruins and that you will once again hear the Angelus ring across the fields at sunset. Remember her, my friends and cousins, pray for her as a saint upon earth, and fight gloriously to help her to success!"

Gordon had restrained himself with difficulty while this scene was being enacted; he could not bear the thought of the King touching the girl's hand. He struggled to prevent himself from crying out at the false position into which he had dragged her; and yet there was something so admirably sincere in the King's words, something so courteous and manly, that it robbed his words of all the theatrical effect they held, and his tribute to the girl filled even Gordon with an emotion which on the part of the young nobles found expression in cheer upon cheer.

Gordon recalled these cheers and the looks of wondering admiration which had been turned upon Miss Carson, and he grew so hot at the recollection that he struck the wall beside him savagely with his clinched fist, and damned the obstinacy of his young and beautiful friend with a sincerity and vigor that was the highest expression of his interest in her behalf.

He threw his cigar into the rampart at his feet and dropped back into the high road. It was deserted at the time, except for the presence of a tall, slightly built stranger, who advanced toward him from the city gates. The man was dressed in garments of European fashion and carried himself like a soldier, and Gordon put him down at a glance as one of the volunteers from Paris. The stranger was walking leisurely, stopping to gaze at the feluccas in the bay, and then turning to look up at the fortress on the hill. He seemed to have no purpose in his walk except the interest of a tourist, and as he drew up even with Gordon he raised his helmet politely and, greeting him in English, asked if he were on the right road to the Bashaw's Palace. Gordon pointed to where the white walls of the palace rose above the other white walls about it.

"That is it," he said. "All the roads lead to it. You keep going up hill."

"Thank you," said the stranger. "I see I have taken a long way." He put his white umbrella in the sand, and, removing his helmet, mopped his forehead with his handkerchief. "It is a curious old town, Tangier," he said, affably, "but too many hills, is it not so? Algiers I like better. There is more life."

"Yes, Algiers is almost as good as the boulevards," Gordon assented, "if you like the boulevards. I prefer this place because it is unspoiled. But, as you say, there is not much to do here."

The stranger's eyes fell upon the Hôtel Grande Bretagne, which stood a quarter of a mile away from them on the beach.

"That is the Hôtel Bretagne, is it not?" he asked. Gordon answered him with a nod.

"The King Louis of Messina, so the chasseur

at the hotel tells me, is stopping there en suite?"
the stranger added, with an interrogative air of
one who volunteers an interesting fact, and who
asks if it is true at the same moment.

"I can't say, I'm sure," Gordon replied. "I
only arrived here yesterday."

The stranger bowed his head in recognition of
this piece of personal information, and, putting on
his helmet, picked up his umbrella as though to
continue his stroll. As he did so his eyes wandered
over the harbor and were arrested with apparent
interest by the yacht, which lay a conspicuous object on the blue water. He pointed at it with his
umbrella.

"One of your English men-of-war is in the harbor, I see. She is very pretty, but not large; not
so large as many," he said.

Gordon turned his head obligingly and gazed
at the yacht with polite interest. "Is that a man-
of-war? I thought it was a yacht," he said. "I'm
not familiar with the English war-vessels. I am
an American."

"Ah, indeed!" commented the affable stranger.
"I am French myself, but I think she is a man-
of-war. I saw her guns when I passed on the
steamer from Gibraltar."

Gordon knew that the steamer did not pass

within half a mile of where the yacht lay at anchor, but he considered it might be possible to see her decks with the aid of a glass.

"You may be right," he answered, indifferently. As he turned his eyes from the boat he saw a woman, dressed in white, and carrying a parasol, leave the gardens of the Hôtel Bretagne, and come toward them along the beach. The Frenchman, following the direction of his eyes, saw her also, and regarded her instantly with such evident concern that Gordon, who had recognized her even at that distance as the Countess Zara, felt assured that his inquisitor held, as he had already suspected, more than a tourist's interest in Tangier.

"Well, I will wish you a good-morning," said the Frenchman, hurriedly.

"Good-morning," Gordon replied, and taking a cigar from his case, he seated himself again upon the rampart. As he walked away the stranger glanced back over his shoulder, but Gordon was apparently absorbed in watching the waves below him, and had lost all interest in his chance acquaintance. But he watched both the woman and the Frenchman as they advanced slowly from opposite directions and drew nearer together, and he was not altogether surprised, when the man was

within twenty feet of her, to see her start and stand
still, and then, with the indecision of a hunted animal, move uncertainly, and then turn and run in
the direction of the hotel.   Something the man apparently called after her caused her to stop, and
Gordon observed them now with undisguised interest as they stood conversing together, oblivious
of the conspicuous mark they made on the broad
white beach under the brilliant sun.

"I wonder what he's up to now?" Gordon
mused.   "He was trying to pump me, that's evident, and he certainly recognized the lady, and she
apparently did not want to recognize him.   I wonder if he is a rejected lover, or another conspirator.
This is a most amusing place, nothing but plots
and counterplots and—Hello!" he exclaimed
aloud.   The man had moved quickly past Madame
Zara, and had started toward the hotel, and Zara
had held out her hand to him, as though to en-
treat him to remain.   But he did not stop, and she
had taken a few uncertain steps after him, and
had then, much to the American's dismay, fallen
limply on her back on the soft sand.   She was not
a hundred yards distant from where he sat, and in
an instant he had slipped from the wall, and
dropped on his hands and knees on the beach below.   When Gordon reached her the Frenchman

had returned, and was supporting her head on his knee and covering her head with her parasol.

"The lady has fainted!" he exclaimed, eagerly. His manner was no longer one of idle indolence. He was wide awake now and visibly excited.

"The sun has been too much for her," he said. "It is most dangerous walking about at this time of day."

Gordon ran down the beach and scooped up some water in his helmet, and dipping his handkerchief in it bathed her temples and cheek. He had time to note that she was a very beautiful girl, and the pallor of her face gave it a touch of gentleness that he had not seen there before.

"I will go to the hotel and bring assistance," said the stranger, uneasily, as the woman showed signs of regaining consciousness.

"No," said Gordon, "you'll stay where you are and shade her with her umbrella. She'll be all right in a minute."

The girl opened her eyes, and looking up saw Gordon bending over her. She regarded him for a moment and made an effort to rise, and in her endeavor to do so her eyes met those of the Frenchman, and with a sharp moan she shut them again and threw herself from Gordon's knee to the sand.

"Give me that umbrella," said Gordon, "and go stand over there out of the way."

The man rose from his knee without showing any resentment and walked some little distance away, where he stood with his arms folded, looking out to sea. He seemed much too occupied with something of personal interest to concern himself with a woman's fainting-spell. The girl lifted herself slowly to her elbow, and then, before Gordon could assist her, rose with a quick, graceful movement and stood erect upon her feet. She placed a detaining hand for an instant on the American's arm.

"Thank you very much," she said. "I am afraid I have been imprudent in going out into the sun." Her eyes were fixed upon the Frenchman, who stood moodily staring at the sea and tearing one of his finger-nails with his teeth. He seemed utterly oblivious of their presence. The girl held out her hand for the parasol she had dropped and took it from Gordon with a bow.

"May I walk back with you to your hotel?" he asked. "Unless this gentleman——"

"Thank you," the girl said, in tones which the Frenchman could have easily overheard had he been listening. "I am quite able to go alone now; it is only a step."

The King's Jackal

She was still regarding the Frenchman closely;
but as he was obviously unconscious of them she
moved so that Gordon hid her from him, and in
an entirely different voice she said, speaking rapidly,—

"You are Mr. Gordon, the American who
joined us last night. That man is a spy from Messina. He is Renauld, the Commander-in-Chief of
their army. He must be gotten away from here
at once. It is a matter for a man to attend to.
Will you do it?"

"How do you know this?" Gordon asked.
"How do you know he is General Renauld? I
want to be certain."

The girl tossed her head impatiently.

"He was pointed out to me at Messina. I saw
him there in command at a review. He has just
spoken to me—that was what frightened me into
that fainting-spell. I didn't think I was so weak,"
she said, shaking her head. "He offered me a
bribe to inform him of our plans. I tell you he
is a spy."

"That's all right," said Gordon, reassuringly;
"you go back to the hotel now and send those
guards here on a run. I'll make a charge against
him and have him locked up until after we sail
to-night. Hurry, please; I'll stay here."

The King's Jackal

Gordon felt a pleasurable glow of excitement. It was his nature to throw himself into everything he did and to at once become a partisan. It was a quality which made his writings attractive to the reader, and an object of concern to his editor. At the very word "spy," and at this first hint of opposition to the cause in which he had but just enlisted, he thrilled as though it had always been his own, and he regarded the Frenchman with a personal dislike as sudden as it was unfounded.

The Frenchman had turned and was walking in the direction of the city gate. His eyes were bent on the sandy beach which stretched before him, and he made his way utterly unmindful of the waves that stole up to his feet and left little pools of water in his path. Gordon beckoned impatiently to the two soldiers who came running toward him at the hotel, and moved forward to meet them the sooner. He took one of them by the wrist and pointed with his other hand at the retreating figure of the Frenchman.

"That man," he said, "is one of the King's enemies. The King is in danger while that man is here. Your duty is to protect the King, so he gives this foreigner into your charge."

The soldier nodded his head in assent.

"The King himself sent us," he replied.

The King's Jackal

"You will place him in the Civil Prison," Gordon continued, "until the King is safe on his yacht, and you will not allow him to send for the French Consul-General. If he sees the Consul-General he will tell him a great many lies about you, and a great war-ship will come and your Bashaw will be forced to pay the foreigners much money. I will go with you and tell this man in his own tongue what you are going to do with him."

They walked hurriedly after the Frenchman, and when they had overtaken him Gordon halted and bowed.

"One moment, please," he said. "These soldiers have an order for your arrest. I speak the language, and if you have anything to say to them I will interpret for you."

The Frenchman stared from Gordon to the guards and then laughed incredulously but with no great confidence. He had much to say, but he demanded to kno first why he should be arrested.

"The lady you insulted," Gordon answered, gravely, "happened, unfortunately for you, to be one of the King's guests. She has complained to him, and he has sent these soldiers to put you where you cannot trouble her again. You see, sir, you cannot annoy women with impunity even in this barbarous country."

95

"Insult her! I did not insult her," the man retorted. "That is not the reason I am arrested."

"You annoyed her so much that she fainted. I saw you," said Gordon, backing away with the evident purpose of abandoning the foreigner to his guards.

"She has lied," the man cried, "either to the King or to me. I do not know which, but I am here to find out. That is why I came to Tangier, and I intend to learn the truth."

"You've begun rather badly," Gordon answered, as he still retreated. "In the Civil Prison your field of investigation will be limited."

The Frenchman took a hasty step toward him, shrugging off the hand one of the soldiers had placed on his shoulder.

"Are you the Prince Kalonay, sir?" he demanded. "But surely not," he added.

"No, I am not the Prince," Gordon answered. "I bid you good-morning, sir."

"Then you are on the other side," the man called after him eagerly, with a tone of great relief. "I have been right from the very first. I see it plainly. It is a double plot, and you are one of that woman's dupes. Listen to me—I beg of you, listen to me—I have a story to tell."

The King's Jackal

Gordon paused and looked back at the man over his shoulder, doubtfully.

"It's like the Arabian Nights," he said, with a puzzled smile. "There was once a rich merchant of Bagdad and the Sultan was going to execute him, but they put off the execution until he could tell them the story of the Beautiful Countess and the French Envoy. I am sorry," he added, shaking his head, "but I cannot listen now. I must not be seen talking to you at all, and everyone can see us here."

They were as conspicuous figures on the flat surface of the beach as two palms in a desert, and Gordon was most anxious to escape, for he was conscious that he could be observed from every point in the town. A hundred yards away, on the terrace of the hotel, he saw the King, Madame Zara, Barrat, and Erhaupt standing together watching them.

"If the American leaves him now, we are safe," the King was saying. He spoke in a whisper, as though he feared that even at that distance Gordon and the Frenchman could overhear his words. "But if he remains with him he will find out the truth, and that means ruin. He will ruin us."

"Look, he is coming this way," Zara answered. "He is leaving him. The danger is past."

The Frenchman raised his eyes and saw the four figures grouped closely together on the terrace.

"See, what did I tell you?" he cried. "She is with the King now. It is a plot within a plot, and I believe you know it," he added, furiously. "You are one of these brave blackmailers yourself—that is why you will not let me speak."

"Blackmailers!" said Gordon. "Confound your impudence, what the devil do you mean by that?"

But the Frenchman was staring angrily at the distant group on the terrace, and Gordon turned his eyes in the same direction. Something he saw in the strained and eager attitude of the four conspirators moved him to a sudden determination.

"That will do, you must go," he commanded, pointing with his arm toward the city gate; and before the Frenchman could reply, he gave an order to the guards, and they seized the foreigner roughly by either arm and hurried him away.

"Thank God!" exclaimed the King, piously. "They have separated, and the boy thinks he is rendering us great service. Well, and so he is, the young fool."

The group on the piazza remained motionless,

watching Gordon as he leisurely lit a cigar and stood looking out at the harbor until the Frenchman had disappeared inside the city wall. Then he turned and walked slowly after him.

"I do not like that. I do not like his following him," said Barrat, suspiciously.

"That is nothing," answered the King. "He is going to play the spy and see that the man is safely in jail. Then he will return and report to us. We must congratulate him warmly. He follows at a discreet distance, you observe, and keeps himself well out of sight. The boy knows better than to compromise himself by being seen in conversation with the man. Of course, if Renauld is set free we must say we had no part in his arrest, that the American made the arrest on his own authority. What a convenient tool the young man is. Why, his coming really frightened us at first, and now—now we make a cat's-paw of him." The King laughed merrily. "We undervalue ourselves sometimes, do we not?"

"He is a nice boy," said Zara. "I feel rather sorry for him. He looked **so anxious and** distressed when I was so silly as to faint on the beach just now. He handled me as tenderly as a woman would have done—not that women have generally handled me tenderly," she added.

"I was thinking the simile was rather misplaced," said the King.

Gordon passed the city wall and heard the gates swing to behind him. The Frenchman and his two captors were just ahead, toiling heavily up the steep and narrow street. Gordon threw his cigar from him and ran leaping over the huge cobbles to the Frenchman's side and touched him on the shoulder.

"We are out of sight of the hotel, now, General," he said. He pointed to the dark, cool recesses of a coffee-shop and held back the rug that hung before it. "Come in here," he said, "and tell me that story."

IV

Baron Barrat was suspicious by education—his experience of life and his own conduct had tended to render him so; and accordingly when, three hours after he had seen Gordon apparently commit the French officer to jail, he found them leaving a café in the most friendly and amicable spirit, he wasted no time in investigation, but hurried at once to warn the King.

"What we feared would happen, has happened," he said. "The Frenchman has told Gordon that Zara and Kalonay sold the secret of the expedition, and Gordon will be coming here to warn you of it. Now, what are you going to do? We must act quickly."

"I shall refuse to believe the Frenchman, of course," said the King. "I shall ask Zara in his presence to answer his charges, and she will tell him he lies. That is all there will be of it. What does it matter what he says? We sail at midnight. We can keep him quiet until then."

"If he is troublesome I can call for help from this room, and the servants of the hotel and the guards will rush in and find us struggling together. We will charge him with an attempt at assassination, and this time he surely will go to jail. By to-morrow morning we shall be many miles at sea."

"But he can cable to Messina, by way of Gibraltar, and head us off," objected Barrat.

"What can he cable?" demanded the King. "Nothing the people of the Republic do not already know. It is our friends here that must not find us out. That is the main thing. Thank Heaven!" he exclaimed, "Kalonay and Paul are out of the way, and those crazy boys from Paris. We will settle it here among ourselves in five minutes."

"And the American?" asked Zara. "He knows, he will come with him. Suppose he believes, suppose he believes that Kalonay and I have sold you out, but suspects that you know it?"

"The American can go to the devil," said the King. "Confound him and his insolence. I'll have him in the prison too, if he interferes. Or Erhaupt can pick a quarrel with him here and fight it out behind the sand-hills before the others get back from their picnic. He has done as much for me before."

Zara stood up. She was trembling slightly, and she glanced fearfully from Erhaupt to the King.

"You will not do that," she said.

"And why not, madame?" demanded Louis.

"Because it will be murder," Zara whispered. "He will murder him as he did that boy in the Park at Pesth."

"What does the woman mean?" growled the German. "Is she mad? Send her to her room, Louis."

"You know what I mean," Zara answered, her voice rising, in her excitement. "You fired before they gave the word. I know you did. Oh, Louis," she cried, "you never warned me it might come to this. I am afraid. I am afraid to meet that man——"

She gave a sudden cry. "And Kalonay!" She held out her hands appealingly. "Indeed," she cried, "do not let Kalonay question me."

"Silence!" commanded the King. "You are acting like a fool." He advanced toward her, and clasped her wrist firmly in his hand. "No nerves, now," he said. "I'll not have it. You shall meet Kalonay, and you shall swear that he is in the plot against me. If you fail us now, we are ruined. As it is, we are sure to lose the bribe from the Republic, but we may still get Miss Carson's money if you play your part. It is your word and the word of the Frenchman against Kalonay's.

And we have the paper signed by you for Kalonay as evidence. Have you got it with you?"

Zara bowed her head. "It is always with me," she answered.

"Good," said the King. "It will be a difficult chance, but if you stand to your story, and we pretend to believe you, the others may believe you, too."

"But I cannot," Zara cried. "I know I cannot. I tell you if you put me face to face with Kalonay, I shall fail you. I shall break down. They will see that I am lying. Send me away. Send me away before they come. Tell them I saw the Frenchman, and suspected I had been found out, and that I have gone away. Tell them you don't know where I am."

"I believe she's right," Erhaupt said. "She will do us more harm than good. Let her go to her room and wait there."

"She will remain where she is," said the King, sternly. "And she will keep her courage and her wits about her, or——"

He was interrupted by an exclamation from Barrat. "Whatever you mean to do, you must do it at once," he said, grimly. He was standing at the window which overlooked the beach. "Here they come now," he continued. "The American has taken no chances, he is bringing an audience with him."

The King and Erhaupt ran to the window, and peered over Barrat's shoulder.

Advancing toward them along the beach, some on foot, and some on horseback, were all the members of the expedition, those who had been of the riding-party and those who had remained in Tangier. Gordon and the Frenchman Renauld were far in the lead, walking by themselves and speaking earnestly together; Father Paul was walking with Mrs. Carson and her daughter, and Kalonay was riding with two of the volunteers, the Count de Rouen and Prince Henri of Poitiers.

When the King and Erhaupt turned from the window the Countess Zara had disappeared. "It is better so," said Erhaupt; "she was so badly frightened she would have told the truth."

The King stood leaning on the back of a large arm-chair. "Well, the moment has come, it is our last chance," he said. "Send for the Crown Prince, Baron. I shall be discovered in the act of taking a tender farewell of my son."

Barrat made an eager gesture of dissent.

"I would not do that," he cried. "If we are to make charges against the Jackal do not have the boy present; the boy must not hear them. You know how Kalonay worships the child, and it would enrage him more to be exposed before the Prince than before all the rest of the world. He will be hard enough to handle without that. Don't try him too far."

"You are absurd, Barrat," exclaimed the King. "The boy won't understand what is said."

"No, but the Jackal will," Barrat returned. "You don't understand him, Louis, he is like a woman; he has sentiment and feelings, and when we all turn on him he will act like a madman. Keep the boy out of his sight, I tell you. It's the only thing he cares for in the world. He has been a better father to him than you ever have been."

"That was quite natural; that was because it was his duty," said the King, calmly. "A Kalonay has always been the protector and tutor of the heir-apparent. If this one chooses to give his heart with his service, that is not my concern. Why, confound them, they all think more of the child than they do of me. That is why I need him by me now."

Barrat shook his head. "I tell you it will make trouble," he persisted. "Kalonay will not stand it. He and the child are more like comrades than a tutor and his pupil. Why, Kalonay would rather sit with the boy in the Champs-Élysées and

point out the people as they go by than drive at
the side of the prettiest woman in Paris. He always treats him as though he saw the invisible
crown upon his head; he will throw over any of
us to stay in the nursery and play tin soldiers with
him. And when he was ill—" Barrat nodded his
head significantly. "You remember."

"That will do," said the King. "We have no
time to consider the finer feelings of the Jackal;
he is to be sacrificed, and that is all there is of it.
The presence of the child may make him more un-
manageable, but it will certainly make it easier for
me. So go, bring the boy here as I bid you."

Barrat left the room and returned immediately,
followed by the Crown Prince and his nurse. The
Prince was a dark, handsome little fellow of four
years. His mother had died when he was born,
and he had never played with children of his own
age, and his face was absurdly wise and wistful;
but it lighted with a sweet and grateful smile when
anyone showed him kindness or sought to arouse
his interest. To the Crown Prince Kalonay was
an awful and wonderful being. He was the one
person who could make him laugh out of pure
happiness and for no reason, as a child should
laugh. And people who had seen them together
asked which of the princes was the older of the

two. When the child entered the room, clinging
to Barrat's finger, he carried in his other hand a
wooden spade and bucket, still damp with sand,
and he was dressed in a shabby blue sailor suit
which left his little legs bare, and exposed the
scratches and bruises of many falls. A few
moments later, when the conspirators entered the
King's salon, preceded by Erhaupt, they found
the boy standing by his father's knee. The King
had his hand upon the child's head, and had been
interrupted apparently in a discourse on the dignity of kingship, for the royal crown of Messina
had been brought out and stood beside him on the
table, and his other hand rested on it reverently.
It was an effective tableau, and the visitors observed it with varying emotions, but with silence.

The King rose, taking his son's hand in his, and
bowed, looking inquiringly from Barrat to the
Prince Kalonay.

"To what do I owe the pleasure of this visit?"
he asked. "Was it discreet of you to come together in this way? But you are most welcome.
Place chairs for the ladies, Barrat."

Kalonay glanced at the others, and they nodded
to him as though to make him their spokesman.
He pointed at Gordon with his cap.

"We are here on the invitation of this gentleman, your Majesty," he said. "He took it upon himself to send after those of us who had gone into the country, and came in person for the others who remained in town. He tells us he has news of the greatest importance to communicate, which he cannot disclose except to you, and in the presence of all of those who are to take part in the expedition. We decided to accompany him here, as he asked us, and to leave it to your Majesty to say whether or not you wished us to remain." Kalonay smiled in apology at the King, and the King answered him with a smile.

"The procedure is perhaps unconventional," the King said, "but in America they move quickly. No doubt our young companion has acted as he thought was for the best. If he has taken a liberty, the nature of his news will probably excuse him. Perhaps, Mr. Gordon," he added, turning to the American, "you had better first tell me what this discovery is, and I will decide whether it is best to discuss it in open council."

Gordon did not appear to be the least disturbed by the criticism Kalonay and the King had passed upon his conduct. He only smiled pleasantly when the King had finished speaking, and showed no inclination to accept a private audience.

"What I have to say, your Majesty," he began,

"is this. I have learned that all the secrets of your expedition have been sold to the Republic of Messina. One of those now present in this room is charged with having sold them. Shall I go on," he asked, "or do you still think it advisable for any-one to leave the room?"

He paused and glanced from the King to the double row of conspirators, who were standing together in a close semicircle facing the King and himself. The instant he ceased speaking there rose from their ranks an outburst of consternation, of anger, and of indignant denial. The King's spirits rose within him at the sound, although he frowned and made a gesture as though to com-mand silence.

"Mr. Gordon, this is a serious charge you make," he said, smiling grimly. "One that may cost you a great deal—it might cost you your life perhaps." He paused significantly, and there was a second outburst, this time from the younger men, which came so suddenly that it was as though Louis had played upon certain chords on a key-board, and the sounds he wanted had answered to his touch.

"Pardon me, that is not the question," said Gor-don. "That I make charges or run risks in mak-ing charges is not important. That your expedition has failed before it has even started is, however, of great importance, at least so it seems to me."

There was a movement in the circle, and Father Paul pushed his way forward from his place beside Miss Carson's chair. He was so greatly moved that when he spoke his voice was harsh and broken. "What is your authority for saying we have failed?" he demanded.

Gordon bowed gravely and turned and pointed to the Frenchman. "This gentleman," he said, "is General Renauld, Commander-in-Chief of the army of Messina. He is my authority. He knows all that you mean to do. If he knows it, it is likely, is it not, that his army and the President of the Republic know it also, and that when we attempt to land they will be waiting for us."

The King silenced the second outburst that followed this by rising and holding up his hand.

"Silence! I believe I can explain," he said. He was smiling, and his bearing was easy and so full of assurance that the exclamations and whispers died away on the instant. "I am afraid I see what has happened," the King said. "But there need be no cause for alarm. This gentleman is, as Mr. Gordon says, the Commander-in-Chief of the Messinian army, and it is true he suspected that an armed force would invade the island. It is not strange that he should have suspected it, and it needed no traitor to enlighten him. The visit of Father Paul and the Prince Kalonay in the yacht, and their speeches inciting the people to rebellion, would have warned the government that an expedition might soon follow. The return of our yacht to this place has no doubt been made known in Messina through the public press, and General Renauld followed the yacht here to learn what he could of our plans—of our intended movements. He came here to spy on us, and as a spy I ordered Mr. Gordon to arrest him this morning on any charge he pleased, and to place him out of our way until after to-night, when we should have sailed. I chose Mr. Gordon tc undertake this service because he happened to speak the language of the country, and it was necessary to deal directly with the local authorities without the intervention of an outsider. What has happened is only too evident. The spy, who when he came here only suspected, now, as Mr. Gordon says, knows the truth, and he could have learned it only from one person, to whom he has no doubt **paid** a pretty price for the information." The King took a step forward and pointed with his hand at the American. "I gave that man into your keeping, sir," he cried, "but I had you watched. Instead of placing him in jail you took him to a café and remained there with him for three hours, and from that café you came directly here to this room. If he knows the truth, he learned it in that café, and he learned it from you!" There was a ring of such earnestness and sincerity in the King's speech, and he delivered it with such indignation and bitter contempt that a shout of relief, of approbation and conviction, went up from his hearers, and fell as quickly on the words as the applause of an audience drowns out the last note of a great burst of song. Barrat, in the excess of his relief, turned his back sharply on the King, glancing sideways at Erhaupt and shaking his head in speechless admiration.

"He is wonderful, simply wonderful," Erhaupt muttered; "he would have made a great actor or a great diplomat."

"He is wasted as a King," whispered Barrat.

There was a menacing movement on the part of the younger men toward Gordon and General Renauld, which the King noted, but which he made no effort to check. Neither Gordon nor General Renauld gave any sign that they observed it. The American was busily engaged in searching his pockets, and from one of these he produced two pieces of paper, which he held up above his head, so that those in the room might see them.

"One moment, please," he began, and then waited until the tumult in the room had ceased. "Again, I must point out to you," he said, in brisk, business-like tones, "that we are digressing. The important thing is not who did, or did not, sell out the expedition, but that it is in danger of failing altogether. What his Majesty says is in part correct. I did not take this gentleman to jail; I did take him to a café, and there he told me much more concerning the expedition than I had learned from those directly interested. His information, he told me, had been sold to the Republic by one who visited the island and who claimed to act for one other. I appreciated the importance of what he said, and I also guessed that my word and his unsupported might be doubted, as you have just doubted it. So I took the liberty of verifying what General Renauld told me by cabling to the President of Messina."

There was a shout of consternation at these words, but Gordon's manner was so confident and the audacity of his admission so surprised his hear·· ers that they were silent again immediately, and waited, with breathless interest, while Gordon unfolded one of the pieces of paper.

"This is a copy of the cablegram I sent the President," he said, "and to which, with his permission, I signed General Renauld's name. It is as follows:—

The President. The Palace, Messina.—They will not believe you are fully informed. Cable at once the exact hour when they will leave Tangier, at what hour they expect to land, at what place they expect to land, what sum you have promised to pay for this information, and the names of those to whom it is to be paid.

RENAULD.

Gordon lowered the paper. "Is that quite clear?" he asked. "Do you follow me? I have invited the enemy himself to inform you of your plans, and to tell you who has betrayed them. His answer, which was received a half hour ago, removes all suspicion from any save those he names. General Renauld and myself cease to be of the least consequence in the matter; we are only messengers. It is the President of Messina who will speak to you now. If you still doubt that the secret of your expedition is known to the President you will have to doubt him."

The King sprang quickly to his feet and struck the arm of his chair sharply with his open hand.

"I shall not permit that message to be read," he said. "If we have a traitor here, he is a traitor against me. And I shall deal with him as I see fit, in private."

There was a murmur of disappointment and of disapproval even, and the King again struck the arm of his chair for silence. Kalonay advanced toward him, shaking his head and holding out his hands in protest.

"Your Majesty, I beseech you," he began. "This concerns us all," he cried. "It is too evident that we have been betrayed; but it is not fair to any of us that we should all lie under suspicion, as we must unless it is told who has been guilty of this infamy. I beg your Majesty to reconsider. There is no one in this room who is not in our secret, and whoever has betrayed us must be with us here and now. I, who have an interest second only to your own, ask that that cablegram be read."

There was a murmur of approbation from the conspirators, and exclamations of approval and entreaty. Miss Carson, in her excitement, had risen to her feet and was standing holding her mother's hand. The King glanced uncertainly at Kalonay, and then turned to Barrat and Erhaupt as if in doubt.

Gordon's eyes were fixed for a moment on Kalonay with a strange and puzzled expression. Then he gave a short sigh of relief, and turning quickly searched the faces of those around him. What he saw seemed to confirm him in his purpose, for he folded the paper and placed it in his pocket. "His Majesty is right," he said. "I shall not read this."

Kalonay and Father Paul turned upon him angrily. "You have no choice in the matter, sir," Kalonay cried. "It has passed entirely out of your hands."

"I beg your Majesty that the cablegram be read," the priest demanded, in a voice that held less the tone of a request than of a command.

"I shall not read it," persisted Gordon, "because the person chiefly concerned is not present."

"That is all the more reason for reading it," said Kalonay. "Your Majesty must reconsider."

The King whispered to Barrat, and the others waited in silence that expressed their interest more clearly than a chorus of questions would have done.

"It shall be as you ask," the King said, at last. "You may read the message, Mr. Gordon."

Gordon opened the paper and looked at it for some seconds of time with a grave and perplexed expression, and then, with a short breath, as one who takes a plunge, read it aloud. "This is it," he said.

To General Renauld. Cable Office, Tangier.— They leave Tangier Tuesday at midnight, they land at daybreak Thursday morning on the south beach below the old breakwater. The secret of the expedition was sold us for three hundred thousand francs by the Countess Zara and the Prince Kalonay.

Gordon stuck the paper in his pocket, and, crossing to Kalonay, held out his hand, with a smile. "I don't believe it, of course," he said; "but you would have it."

Kalonay neither saw the gesture nor heard the words. He was turning in bewilderment from the King to Father Paul, and he laughed uncertainly.

"What nonsense is this?" he demanded. "Whose sorry trick is this? The lie is not even ingenious."

General Renauld had not spoken since he had entered the room, but now he advanced in front of Kalonay and faced him with a threatening gesture.

"The President of Messina does not lie, sir," he said, sternly. "I myself saw the Countess Zara write out that paper, which I and others signed, and in which we agreed to pay to her and to you the money you asked for betraying your King."

Father Paul pressed his hand heavily on Kalonay's shoulder. "Do not answer him," he commanded. Gordon had moved to Kalonay's other side, and the three men had unconsciously assumed an attitude of defence, and stood back to back in a little group facing the angry circle that ecompassed them. The priest raised his arm to command a hearing.

"Where is Madam Zara?" he cried.

"Ah, where indeed?" echoed the King, sinking back into his chair. "She has fled. It is all too evident now; she has betrayed us and she has fled."

But on his words, as if in answer to the priest's summons, the curtains that hid the door into the King's private room were pulled to one side, and Madame Zara appeared between them, glancing fearfully at the excited crowd before her. As she stood hesitating on the threshold, she swayed slightly and clutched the curtains for a moment as though for support. The priest advanced, and led her to the centre of the room. She held a folded paper in her hand, which she gave to him in silence

"You have heard what has passed?" he asked, with a toss of his head toward the heavy curtains. The woman raised her head and bowed. The priest unfolded the paper.

"Am I to read this?" he asked. The woman bowed again.

There was silence in the room while the priest's eyes ran quickly over the paper. He crushed it in his hand.

"It is as General Renauld says," he exclaimed. "In this the Republic of Messina agrees to pay the Countess Zara and the Prince Kalonay three hundred thousand francs, if the expedition is withdrawn after it has made a pretence of landing on the shores of Messina."

He took a step forward. "Madame Zara," he cried, in a tone of warning, "do you pretend that the Prince Kalonay was your accomplice in this; that he knew what you meant to do?"

Madame Zara once more bowed her head.

"No! You must speak," commanded the priest. "Answer me!"

Zara hesitated, in evident distress, and glanced appealingly at the King; but the expression on his face was one of grief and of unrelenting virtue.

"I do," she said, at last, in a low voice. "Kalonay did know. He thought the revolution would

not succeed; he thought it would fail, and so—
and so—and we needed money. They made me—
I, O my God, I cannot—I cannot!" she cried, suddenly, sinking on her knees and hiding her face
with her hands.

Kalonay stepped toward her and lifted her
gently to her feet; but when she looked and saw
who it was that held her, she gave a cry and pulled
herself free. She staggered and would have
fallen, had not Gordon caught and held her by the
arm. The King rose from his chair and pointed
at the shrinking figure of the woman.

"Stand aside from her," he said, sternly. "Why
should we pity her, what pity has she shown for
us—for me? She has robbed me of my inheri-
tance. But let her go, she is a woman; we cannot
punish her. Her sins rest on her own head. But
you—you," he cried, turning fiercely on Kalonay,
his voice rising to a high and melancholy key,
"you whom I have heaped with honors, whom I
have leaned upon as on the arm of a brother, that
you should have sold me for silver, that you should
have turned Judas!"

The crowd of volunteers, bewildered by the
rapid succession of events, and confused and ren-
dered desperate by the failure of their expedition,
caught up the word, and pressing forward with a

rush, surrounded Kalonay in an angry circle, crying "Judas!" "Traitor!" and "Coward!"

Kalonay turned from side to side. On some he
smiled bitterly in silence, and at others he broke
out into swift and fierce denunciations; but the men
around him crowded closer and would not permit
him to be heard. He had turned upon them, again
challenging them to listen, when there was an
opening in the circle and the men stepped back,
and Miss Carson pushed her way among them and
halted at Kalonay's side. She did not look at him,
but at the men about him. She was the only calm
figure in the group, and her calmness at such a
crisis, and her youth, and the fineness and fearlessness of her beauty, surprised them into a sudden
quiet. There was instantly a cry for order, and
the men stood curious and puzzled, watching to
see what she would do.

"Gentlemen," she said, in a clear, grave voice.
"Gentlemen," she repeated, sharply, as a few mur-
murs still greeted her, "if you are gentlemen, let
this lady speak. She has not finished." She
crossed quickly and took the Countess Zara by the
hand. "Go on, madame," she urged, gently. "Do
not be afraid. You say they made you do it. Who
made you do it? You have told us a part of the
truth. Now tell us the whole truth." For a mo-

ment the girl seemed much the older of the two, and as Zara glanced up at her fearfully, she smiled to reassure her, and stroked the woman's hand with her own. "Who made you do it?" she repeated. "Not the Prince Kalonay, surely. You cannot hope to make us believe that. We trust him absolutely. Who was it, then?"

The King sprang forward with an oath; his apathy and mock dignity had fallen from him like a mask. His face was mottled, and his vicious little eyes flashed with fear and anger. Erhaupt crowded close behind him, crouching like a dog at his heels.

"She has lied enough already," the King cried. "We will not listen to her. Take her away."

"Yes, let her go," shouted Erhaupt, with a laugh. "If she had been a decent woman——"

There was a quick parting in the group and the sound of a heavy blow as Kalonay flung himself upon Erhaupt and struck him in the face, so that he staggered and fell at length upon the floor. Gordon stood over him, his fingers twitching at his side.

"Stand up, you bully," he said, "and get out of this, before we throw you out."

Zara's face had turned a pitiful crimson, but her eyes flashed and burned with resolve and indignation. She stood erect and menacing, like an angry goddess, and more beautiful in her indignation than they had ever seen her.

"Now, I shall tell them the truth," she said, sternly. "That man," she cried, pointing her finger at the King, "that man whom they call a King—that man who would have sacrificed the only friend who serves him unselfishly—is the man who sold your secret to the enemy. It was he who made me do it. He sent me to Messina, and while the priest and the Prince Kalonay were working in the south, I sold them to the government at the capital. Barrat knew it, Erhaupt knew it, the King himself planned it—to get money. He has robbed all of his own people; he had meant to rob this young girl; and he is so mean and pitiful a creature that to save himself **he now** tries to hide behind the skirts of a woman, and to sacrifice her, —the woman who has given her soul to him. And for this—my God!" she cried, her voice rising in an accent of agony and bitter contempt— "for this!"

There was a grim and momentous silence in the room while Zara turned, and without waiting to learn what effect her words might have, made her way swiftly through the crowd and passed on out of the room and on to the terrace beyond.

The King's Jackal

The King crouched back in his chair like a common criminal in the dock, glancing fearfully from under his lowered eyebrows at the faces about him, and on none did he see the least question of doubt but that Zara had at last spoken the truth.

"She lies," the King muttered, as though answering their unspoken thoughts, "the woman lies."

There was no movement from the men about him. Shame for him, and grief and bitter disappointment for themselves, showed on the face of each. From outside a sea-breeze caught up the sand of the beach and drove it whispering against the high windows, and the beat of the waves upon the shores filled out and marked the silence of the room.

The Prince Kalonay stepped from the circle and stood for a moment before the King, regarding him with an expression of grief and bitter irony. The King's eyes rose insolently, and faltered, and sank.

"For many years, your Majesty," the Prince said, but so solemnly that it was as though he were a judge upon the bench, or a priest speaking across an open grave, "the Princes of my house have served the Kings of yours. In times of war they fought for the King in battle, they beggared themselves for him in times of peace; our women sold their jewels for the King, our men gave him their lives, and in all of these centuries the story of their loyalty, of their devotion, has had but one sequel, and has met with but one reward,—ingratitude and selfishness and treachery. You know how I have served you, Louis. You know that I gave up my fortune and my home to go into exile with you, and I did that gladly. But I did more than that. I did more than any king or any man has the right to expect of any other man. I served your idle purposes so well that you, yourself, called me your Jackal, the only title your Majesty has ever bestowed that was deserved. There is no low thing nor no base thing that I have not done for you. To serve your pleasures, to gain you money, I have sunken so low that all the royal blood in Europe could not make me clean. But there is a limit to what a man may do for his King, and to the loyalty a King may have the right to demand. And to-day and here, with me, the story of our devotion to your House ends, and you go your way and I go mine, and the last of my race breaks his sword and throws it at your feet, and is done with you and yours forever."

Even those in the room who held no sympathy

in their hearts for the sentiment that had inspired
the young man, felt that at that moment and in
their hearing he had renounced what was to him
his religion and his faith, and on the faces of all
was the expression of a deep pity and concern.
Their own adventure, in the light of his grief and
bitterness of spirit, seemed selfish and little, and
they stood motionless, in an awed and sorrowful
silence.

The tense strain of the moment was broken suddenly by the advent on the scene of an actor who
had, in the rush of events, been neglected and forgotten. The little Crown Prince had stood clinging to his nurse's skirts, an uncomprehending spec-
tator of what was going forward. But he now advanced slowly, feeling that the silence invited him
to claim his father's notice. He halted beside the
chair in which Louis sat, his head bent on his
hands, and made an effort to draw himself up to
his father's knee.

But the King pushed him down, and hid his face
from him. The child turned irresolutely, with a
troubled countenance, and, looking up, saw that
the attention of all was fixed upon him. At this
discovery a sudden flood of shyness overtook him,
and he retreated hastily until his eyes fell on the
Prince Kalonay, standing alone, with his own eyes

turned resolutely away. There was a breathless
hush in the room as the child, with a happy sigh,
ran to his former friend and comrade, and reached
up both his arms. The tableau was a familiar one
to those who knew them, and meant only that the
child asked to be lifted up and swung to the man's
shoulder; but following as it did on what had just
passed, the gesture and the attitude carried with
them the significance of an appeal. Kalonay, as
though with a great effort, lowered his eyes to the
upturned face of the child below him, but held
himself back and stood stiffly erect. A sharp shake
of the head, as though he argued with himself,
was the only sign he gave of the struggle that was
going on within him.

At this second repulse, the child's arms dropped
to his side, his lips quivered, and he stood, a lonely
little figure, glancing up at the circle of men about
him, and struggling to press back the tears that
came creeping to his eyes.

Kalonay regarded him steadfastly for a brief
moment, as though he saw him as a stranger,
searching his face with eyes as pitiful as the child's
own; and then, with a sudden, sharp cry, the
Prince dropped on his knee and caught the child
toward him, crushing him against his heart, and
burying his face on his shoulder. There was a

shout of exultation from the nobles, and an uttered
prayer from the priest, and in a moment the young
men had crowded in around them, struggling to
be the first to kiss the child's hands, and to ask
pardon of the man who held him in his arms.

"Gentlemen," Kalonay cried, his voice laughing
through his tears, "we shall still sail for the island
of Messina. They shall not say of us that we
visited the sins of the father on a child. I was
weak, my friends, and I was credulous. I thought
I could break the tradition of centuries. But our
instincts are stronger than our pride, and the
House I have always served I shall serve to the
last." He swung the Crown Prince high upon his
shoulder, and held his other arm above his head.
"You will help me place this child upon his
throne," he commanded, and the room rang with
cheers. "You will appeal to his people," he cried.
"Do you not think they will rise to this standard-
bearer, will they not rally to his call? For he is
a true Prince, my comrades, who comes to them
with no stain of wrong or treachery, without a
taint, as untarnished as the white snow that lies
summer and winter in the hollow of our hills, 'and
a child shall lead us, and a child shall set them
free.' To the yacht!" he shouted. "We will sail
at once, and while they wait for us to be betrayed

into their hands at the north, we shall be landing in the south, and thousands will be hurrying to our standard."

His last words were lost in a tumult of cheers and cries, and the young men poured out upon the terrace, running toward the shore, and filling the soft night-air with shouts of "Long live the Prince Regent!" "Long live our King!"

As the room grew empty Kalonay crossed it swiftly and advancing to Miss Carson took her hand. His face was radiant with triumph and content. He regarded her steadily for a moment, as though he could not find words to tell his feelings.

"You had faith in me," he said, at last. "Can I ever make you understand how much that means to me? When all had turned against me you trusted me, you had faith in me, in the King's Jackal."

"Silence; you must never say that again," the girl commanded, gently. "You have shown it to be the lie it always was. We shall call you the Defender of the Faith now; you are the guardian of a King." She smiled at the little boy in his arms, and made a slight courtesy to them both. "You have outgrown your old title," she said; "you have a proud one now, you will be the Prince Regent."

Kalonay, with the child in his arms, and Miss

The King's Jackal

Carson were standing quite alone. General Renauld had been led away, guarded by a merry band of youngsters; the King still crouched in his chair, with Barrat bowed behind him, but pulling, with philosophic calm, on a cigarette, and Father Paul and Gordon were in close conversation with Mrs. Carson at the farther end of the room. The sun had set, and the apartment was in semi-darkness. Kalonay moved closer to Miss Carson and looked boldly into her eyes. "There is a prouder title than that of the Regent," he whispered; "will you ever give it me?"

The girl started, breathing quickly, and turned her head aside, making an effort to free her hand, but Kalonay held it closer in his own. "Will you give it me?" he begged.

Then the girl looked up at him smiling, but with such confidence and love in her eyes that he read his answer, though she shook her head, as though to belie the truth her eyes had told him.

"When you have done your work," she said, "come to me or send for me, and I shall come and give you my answer; and whether you fail or succeed the answer will be the same."

Kalonay stooped quickly and kissed her hand, and when he raised his face his eyes were smiling with such happiness that the little child in his arms

read it there, and smiled too in sympathy, and
pressed his face closer against his comrade's shoulder.

Gordon at this moment moved across the room
and bowed, making a deep obeisance to the child.

"Might I be permitted," he asked, "to kiss his
Royal Highness? I should like to boast of the
fact, later," he explained.

The Crown Prince turned his sad, wise eyes on
him in silence, and gravely extended a little hand.

"You may kiss his Highness's hand," said Kalonay, smiling.

Gordon laughed and pressed the fingers in his
own.

"When you talk like that, Kalonay," he said,
"you make me feel like Alice in the court-room
with the Kings and Queens around her. A dozen
times this afternoon I've felt like saying, 'After
all, they are only a pack of cards.'"

Kalonay shook his head and glanced toward
Miss Carson for enlightenment.

"I don't understand," he said.

"No, you couldn't be expected to," said Gordon; "you have not been educated up to that. It
is the point of view."

He stuck out the middle finger of his hand, and
drove it three times deliberately into the side of the

Crown Prince. The child gasped and stared open-mouthed at the friendly stranger, and then catching the laugh in Gordon's eyes, laughed with him.

"Now," said Gordon, "I shall say that I have dug the King of Messina in the ribs—that is even better than having kissed him. God bless your Royal Highness," he said, bowing gravely. "You may find me disrespectful at times," he added; "but then, you must remember, I am going to risk a valuable life for you. At least it's an extremely valuable one to me."

Kalonay looked at Gordon for a moment with serious consideration, and then held out his hand. "You also had faith in me," he said. "I thank you. Are you in earnest; do you really wish to serve us?"

"I mean to stay by you until the boy is crowned," said the American, "unless we separate on our several paths of glory—where they will lead depends, I imagine, on how we have lived."

"Or on how we die," Kalonay added. "I am glad to hear you speak so. If you wish, I shall attach you to the person of the Crown Prince. You shall be on the staff with the rank of Colonel."

Gordon made a low and sweeping bow.

"Rise, Sir Archibald Gordon," he said. "I thank you," he added. "We shall strive to please."

Miss Carson shook her head at him, and sighed in protest.

"Will you always take everything as a joke, Archie?" she said.

"My dear Patty," he answered, "the situation is much too serious to take in any other way."

They moved to the door, and there the priest and Mrs. Carson joined them; but on the threshold Kalonay stopped and looked for the first time since he had addressed him at the King.

He regarded him for some seconds sternly in silence, and then pointed, with his free hand, at the crown of Messina, which still rested on the table at the King's elbow. "Colonel Gordon," he said, in a tone of assured authority, "I give the crown of Messina into your keeping. You will convey it, with all proper regard for its dignity, safely on board the yacht, and then bring it at once to me."

When he had finished speaking the Prince turned and, without looking at the King, passed on with the others across the terrace and disappeared in the direction of the shore, where the launch lay waiting.

Gordon crossed the room and picked up the crown from the table, lifting it with both hands, the King and Barrat watching him in silence as he did so. He hesitated, and held it for a moment, regarding it with much the same expression of awe and amusement that a man shows when he is permitted to hold a strange baby in his arms. Turning, he saw the sinister eyes of the King and of Barrat fastened upon him, and he smiled awkwardly, and in some embarrassment turned the crown about in his hands, so that the jewels in its circle gleamed dully in the dim light of the room. Gordon raised the crown and balanced it on his finger-tips, regarding it severely and shaking his head.

"There are very few of these left in the world now, your Majesty," he said, cheerfully, "and the number is getting smaller every year. We have none at all in my country, and I should think— seeing they are so few—that those who have them would take better care of them, and try to keep them untarnished, and brushed up, and clean." He turned his head and looked inquiringly at the King, but Louis made no sign that he heard him.

"I have no desire, you understand me," continued Gordon, unabashed, "to take advantage of a man when he is down, but the temptation to say 'I told you so' seems almost impossible to resist. What?" he asked—"I beg your pardon, I thought you spoke." But the King continued scornfully silent, and only a contemptuous snort from Barrat expressed his feelings.

Gordon placed the crown carefully under his arm, and then removed it quickly, with a guilty look of dismay at its former owner, and let it swing from his hand; but this fashion of carrying it seemed also lacking in respect, so he held it up again with both hands and glanced at the King in some perplexity.

"There ought to be a sofa-cushion to go with this, or something to carry it on," he said, in a grieved tone. "You see, I am new at this sort of thing. Perhaps your Majesty would kindly give me some expert information. How do you generally carry it?"

The King's eyes snapped open and shut again.

"On my head," he said, grimly.

Gordon laughed in great relief.

"Now, do you know, I like that," he cried. "That shows spirit. I am glad to see you take it so cheerfully. Well, I must be going, sir," he added, nodding, and moving toward the door. "Don't be discouraged. As someone says, 'It's always morning somewhere,' and in my country there's just as good men out of office as there are in it. Good-night."

The King's Jackal

While the sound of Gordon's footsteps died away across the marble terrace, the King and Barrat remained motionless and silent. The darkness in the room deepened and the silence seemed to deepen with it; and still they remained immovable, two shadowy figures in the deserted apartment where the denunciations of those who had abandoned them still seemed to hang and echo in the darkness. What thoughts passed through their minds or for how long a time they might still have sat in bitter contemplation can only be guessed, for they were surprised by the sharp rattle of a lock, the two great doors of the adjoining room were thrown wide open, and a broad and brilliant light flooded the apartment. Niccolas, the King's major-domo, stood between the doors, a black silhouette against the glare of many candles.

"His Majesty is served!" he said.

The King lifted his head sharply, as though he found some lurking mockery in the words, or some fresh affront; but in the obsequious bow of his major-domo there was no mockery, and the table beyond glistened with silver, while a pungent and convincing odor of rich food was wafted insidiously through the open doors.

The King rose with a gentle sigh, and nodded to his companion.

"Come, Barrat," he said, taking the baron's arm in his. "The rascals have robbed us of our throne, but, thank God, they have had the grace to leave me my appetite."

THE REPORTER WHO MADE HIMSELF KING

The Reporter Who Made Himself King

THE Old Time Journalist will tell you that the best reporter is the one who works his way up. He holds that the only way to start is as a printer's devil or as an office boy, to learn in time to set type, to graduate from a compositor into a stenographer, and as a stenographer take down speeches at public meetings, and so finally grow into a real reporter, with a fire badge on your left suspender, and a speaking acquaintance with all the greatest men in the city, not even excepting Police Captains.

That is the old time journalist's idea of it. That is the way he was trained, and that is why at the age of sixty he is still a reporter. If you train up a youth in this way, he will go into reporting with too full a knowledge of the newspaper business, with no illusions concerning it, and with no ignorant enthusiasms, but with a keen and justifiable impression that he is not paid enough for what he does. And he will only do what he is paid to do.

The Reporter Who

Now, you cannot pay a good reporter for what he does, because he does not work for pay. He works for his paper. He gives his time, his health, his brains, his sleeping hours, and his eating hours, and sometimes his life, to get news for it. He thinks the sun rises only that men may have light by which to read it. But if he has been in a newspaper office from his youth up, he finds out before he becomes a reporter that this is not so, and loses his real value. He should come right out of the University where he has been doing "campus notes" for the college weekly, and be pitchforked out into city work without knowing whether the Battery is at Harlem or Hunter's Point, and with the idea that he is a Moulder of Public Opinion and that the Power of the Press is greater than the Power of Money, and that the few lines he writes are of more value in the Editor's eyes than is the column of advertising on the last page, which they are not.

After three years—it is sometimes longer, sometimes not so long—he finds out that he has given his nerves and his youth and his enthusiasm in exchange for a general fund of miscellaneous knowledge, the opportunity of personal encounter with all the greatest and most remarkable men and events that have risen in those three years, and a great fund of resource and patience. He will find that he has crowded the experiences of the lifetime of the ordinary young business man, doctor, or lawyer, or man about town, into three short years; that he has learned to think and to act quickly, to be patient and unmoved when everyone else has lost his head, actually or figuratively speaking; to write as fast as another man can talk, and to be able to talk with authority on matters of which other men do not venture even to think until they have read what he has written with a copy-boy at his elbow on the night previous.

It is necessary for you to know this, that you may understand what manner of man young Albert Gordon was.

Young Gordon had been a reporter just three years. He had left Yale when his last living relative died, and had taken the morning train for New York, where they had promised him reportorial work on one of the innumerable Greatest New York Dailies. He arrived at the office at noon, and was sent back over the same road on which he had just come, to Spuyten Duyvil, where a train had been wrecked and everybody of consequence to suburban New York killed. One of the old reporters hurried him to the office again with his "copy," and after he had delivered that, he was sent to the Tombs to talk French to a man in Murderers' Row, who could not talk anything else, but who had shown some international skill in the use of a jimmy. And at eight, he covered a flower-show in Madison Square Garden; and at eleven was sent over the Brooklyn Bridge in a cab to watch a fire and make guesses at the losses to the insurance companies.

He went to bed at one, and dreamed of shattered locomotives, human beings lying still with blankets over them, rows of cells, and banks of beautiful flowers nodding their heads to the tunes of the brass band in the gallery. He decided when he awoke the next morning that he had entered upon a picturesque and exciting career, and as one day followed another, he became more and more convinced of it, and more and more devoted to it. He was twenty then, and he was now twenty-three, and in that time had become a great reporter, and had been to Presidential conventions in Chicago, revolutions in Hayti, Indian outbreaks on the Plains, and midnight meetings of moonlighters in Tennessee, and had seen what work earthquakes, floods, fire, and fever could do in great cities, and had contradicted the President, and borrowed matches from burglars. And now he thought he would like to rest and breathe a bit, and not to work again unless as a war correspondent. The only obstacle to his becoming a great war correspondent lay in the fact that there was no war, and a war correspondent without a war is about as absurd an individual as a general without an army. He read the papers every morning on the elevated trains for war clouds; but though there were many war clouds, they always drifted apart, and peace smiled again. This was very disappointing to young Gordon, and he became more and more keenly discouraged.

And then as war work was out of the question, he decided to write his novel. It was to be a novel of New York life, and he wanted a quiet place in which to work on it. He was already making inquiries among the suburban residents of his acquaintance for just such a quiet spot, when he received an offer to go to the Island of Opeki in the North Pacific Ocean, as secretary to the American consul at that place. The gentleman who had been appointed by the President to act as consul at Opeki was Captain Leonard T. Travis, a veteran of the Civil War, who had contracted a severe attack of rheumatism while camping out at night in the dew, and who on account of this souvenir of his efforts to save the Union had allowed the Union he had saved to support him in one office or another ever since. He had met young Gordon at a dinner, and had had the presumption to ask him to serve as his secretary, and Gordon, much to his surprise, had accepted his offer. The idea of a quiet life in the tropics with new and beautiful surroundings, and with nothing to do and plenty of time in which to do it, and to write his novel besides, seemed to Albert to be just what he wanted; and though he did not know nor care much for his superior officer, he agreed to go with him promptly, and proceeded to say good-by to his friends and to make his preparations. Captain Travis was so delighted with getting such a clever young gentleman for his secretary, that he referred to him to his friends as "my attaché of legation;" nor did he lessen that gentleman's dignity by telling anyone that the attaché's salary was to be five hundred dollars a year. His own salary was only fifteen hundred dollars; and though his brother-in-law, Senator Rainsford, tried his best to get the amount raised, he was unsuccessful. The consulship to Opeki was instituted early in the '50's, to get rid of and reward a third or fourth cousin of the President's, whose services during the campaign were important, but whose after-presence was embarrassing. He had been created consul to Opeki as being more distant and unaccessible than

any other known spot, and had lived and died
there; and so little was known of the island, and so
difficult was communication with it, that no one
knew he was dead, until Captain Travis, in his
hungry haste for office, had uprooted the sad fact.
Captain Travis, as well as Albert, had a secondary
reason for wishing to visit Opeki. His physician
had told him to go to some warm climate for his
rheumatism, and in accepting the consulship his object was rather to follow out his doctor's orders at
his country's expense, than to serve his country at
the expense of his rheumatism.

Albert could learn but very little of Opeki; nothing, indeed, but that it was situated about one hundred miles from the Island of Octavia, which isl-
and, in turn, was simply described as a coaling-
station three hundred miles distant from the coast
of California. Steamers from San Francisco to
Yokohama stopped every third week at Octavia,
and that was all that either Captain Travis or his
secretary could learn of their new home. This was
so very little, that Albert stipulated to stay only as
long as he liked it, and to return to the States
within a few months if he found such a change of
plan desirable.

As he was going to what was an almost undis-
covered country, he thought it would be advisable

to furnish himself with a supply of articles with which he might trade with the native Opekians, and for this purpose he purchased a large quantity of brass rods, because he had read that Stanley did so, and added to these, brass curtain-chains, and about two hundred leaden medals similar to those sold by street pedlers during the Constitutional Centennial celebration in New York City.

He also collected even more beautiful but less expensive decorations for Christmas-trees, at a wholsesale house on Park Row. These he hoped to exchange for furs or feathers or weapons, or for whatever other curious and valuable trophies the Island of Opeki boasted. He already pictured his rooms on his return hung fantastically with crossed spears and boomerangs, feather head-dresses, and ugly idols.

His friends told him that he was doing a very foolish thing, and argued that once out of the newspaper world, it would be hard to regain his place in it. But he thought the novel that he would write while lost to the world at Opeki would serve to make up for his temporary absence from it, and he expressly and impressively stipulated that the editor should wire him if there was a war.

Captain Travis and his secretary crossed the continent without adventure, and took passage from San Francisco on the first steamer that touched at Octavia. They reached that island in three days, and learned with some concern that there was no regular communication with Opeki, and that it would be necessary to charter a sailboat for the trip. Two fishermen agreed to take them and their trunks, and to get them to their destination within sixteen hours if the wind held good. It was a most unpleasant sail. The rain fell with calm, unrelentless persistence from what was apparently a clear sky; the wind tossed the waves as high as the mast and made Captain Travis ill; and as there was no deck to the big boat, they were forced to huddle up under pieces of canvas, and talked but little. Captain Travis complained of frequent twinges of rheumatism, and gazed forlornly over the gunwale at the empty waste of water.

"If I've got to serve a term of imprisonment on a rock in the middle of the ocean for four years," he said, "I might just as well have done something first to deserve it. This is a pretty way to treat a man who bled for his country. This is gratitude, this is." Albert pulled heavily on his pipe, and wiped the rain and spray from his face and smiled.

"Oh, it won't be so bad when we get there," he

said; "they say these Southern people are always hospitable, and the whites will be glad to see anyone from the States."

"There will be a round of diplomatic dinners," said the consul, with an attempt at cheerfulness. "I have brought two uniforms to wear at them."

It was seven o'clock in the evening when the rain ceased, and one of the black, half-naked fishermen nodded and pointed at a little low line on the horizon.

"Opeki," he said. The line grew in length until it proved to be an island with great mountains rising to the clouds, and, as they drew nearer and nearer, showed a level coast running back to the foot of the mountains and covered with a forest of palms. They next made out a village of thatched huts around a grassy square, and at some distance from the village a wooden structure with a tin roof.

"I wonder where the town is," asked the consul, with a nervous glance at the fishermen. One of them told him that what he saw was the town.

"That?" gasped the consul. "Is that where all the people on the island live?"

The fisherman nodded; but the other added that there were other natives further back in the mountains, but that they were bad men who fought and

ate each other. The consul and his attaché of
legation gazed at the mountains with unspoken
misgivings. They were quite near now, and could
see an immense crowd of men and women, all of
them black, and clad but in the simplest garments,
waiting to receive them. They seemed greatly excited and ran in and out of the huts, and up and
down the beach, as wildly as so many black ants.
But in the front of the group they distinguished
three men who they could see were white, though
they were clothed, like the others, simply in a shirt
and a short pair of trousers. Two of these three
suddenly sprang away on a run and disappeared
among the palm-trees; but the third one, when he
recognized the American flag in the halyards,
threw his straw hat in the water and began turning handsprings over the sand.

"That young gentleman, at least," said Albert,
gravely, "seems pleased to see us."

A dozen of the natives sprang into the water
and came wading and swimming toward them,
grinning and shouting and swinging their arms.

"I don't think it's quite safe, do you?" said the
consul, looking out wildly to the open sea. "You
see, they don't know who I am."

A great black giant threw one arm over the gunwale and shouted something that sounded as if it

were spelt Owah, Owah, as the boat carried him through the surf.

"How do you do?" said Gordon, doubtfully. The boat shook the giant off under the wave and beached itself so suddenly that the American consul was thrown forward to his knees. Gordon did not wait to pick him up, but jumped out and shook hands with the young man who had turned handsprings, while the natives gathered about them in a circle and chatted and laughed in delighted excitement.

"I'm awfully glad to see you," said the young man, eagerly. "My name's Stedman. I'm from New Haven, Connecticut. Where are you from?"

"New York," said Albert. "This," he added, pointing solemnly to Captain Travis, who was still on his knees in the boat, "is the American consul to Opeki." The American consul to Opeki gave a wild look at Mr. Stedman of New Haven and at the natives.

"See here, young man," he gasped, "is this all there is of Opeki?"

"The American consul?" said young Stedman, with a gasp of amazement, and looking from Albert to Captain Travis. "Why, I never supposed they would send another here; the last one died about fifteen years ago, and there hasn't been one since. I've been living in the consul's office with the Bradleys, but I'll move out, of course. I'm sure I'm awfully glad to see you. It'll make it so much more pleasant for me."

"Yes," said Captain Travis, bitterly, as he lifted his rheumatic leg over the boat; "that's why we came."

Mr. Stedman did not notice this. He was too much pleased to be anything but hospitable. "You are soaking wet, aren't you?" he said; "and hungry, I guess. You come right over to the consul's office and get on some other things."

He turned to the natives and gave some rapid orders in their language, and some of them jumped into the boat at this, and began to lift out the trunks, and others ran off toward a large, stout old native, who was sitting gravely on a log, smoking, with the rain beating unnoticed on his gray hair.

"They've gone to tell the King," said Stedman; "but you'd better get something to eat first, and then I'll be happy to present you properly."

"The King," said Captain Travis, with some awe; "is there a king?"

"I never saw a king," Gordon remarked, "and I'm sure I never expected to see one sitting on a log in the rain."

"He's a very good king," said Stedman, confidentially; "and though you mightn't think it to look at him, he's a terrible stickler for etiquette and form. After supper he'll give you an audience; and if you have any tobacco, you had better give him some as a present, and you'd better say it's from the President: he doesn't like to take presents from common people, he's so proud. The only reason he borrows mine is because he thinks I'm the President's son."

"What makes him think that?" demanded the consul, with some shortness. Young Mr. Stedman looked nervously at the consul and at Albert, and said that he guessed someone must have told him.

The consul's office was divided into four rooms with an open court in the middle, filled with palms, and watered somewhat unnecessarily by a fountain.

"I made that," said Stedman, in a modest, offhand way. "I made it out of hollow bamboo reeds connected with a spring. And now I'm making one for the King. He saw this and had a lot of bamboo sticks put up all over the town, without any underground connections, and couldn't make out why the water wouldn't spurt out of them. And because mine spurts, he thinks I'm a magician."

"I Never Saw a King," Gordon Remarked.

Made Himself King

"I suppose," grumbled the consul, "someone told him that too."

"I suppose so," said Mr. Stedman, uneasily.

There was a veranda around the consul's office, and inside the walls were hung with skins, and pictures from illustrated papers, and there was a good deal of bamboo furniture, and four broad, cool-looking beds. The place was as clean as a kitchen. "I made the furniture," said Stedman, "and the Bradleys keep the place in order."

"Who are the Bradleys?" asked Albert.

"The Bradleys are those two men you saw with me," said Stedman; "they deserted from a British man-of-war that stopped here for coal, and they act as my servants. One is Bradley, Sr., and the other Bradley, Jr."

"Then vessels do stop here occasionally?" the consul said, with a pleased smile.

"Well, not often," said Stedman. "Not so very often; about once a year. The Nelson thought this was Octavia, and put off again as soon as she found out her mistake, but the Bradleys took to the bush, and the boat's crew couldn't find them. When they saw your flag, they thought you might mean to send them back, so they ran off to hide again; they'll be back, though, when they get hungry."

The supper young Stedman spread for his guests, as he still treated them, was very refreshing and very good. There was cold fish and pigeon-pie, and a hot omelet filled with mushrooms and olives and tomatoes and onions all sliced up together, and strong black coffee. After supper, Stedman went off to see the King, and came back in a little while to say that his Majesty would give them an audience the next day after breakfast. "It is too dark now," Stedman explained; "and it's raining so that they can't make the street-lamps burn. Did you happen to notice our lamps? I invented them; but they don't work very well yet. I've got the right idea, though, and I'll soon have the town illuminated all over, whether it rains or not."

The consul had been very silent and indifferent, during supper, to all around him. Now he looked up with some show of interest.

"How much longer is it going to rain, do you think?" he asked.

"Oh, I don't know," said Stedman, critically. "Not more than two months, I should say." The consul rubbed his rheumatic leg and sighed, but said nothing.

The Bradleys returned about ten o'clock, and came in very sheepishly. The consul had gone

off to pay the boatmen who had brought them, and
Albert in his absence assured the sailors that there
was not the least danger of their being sent away.
Then he turned into one of the beds, and Stedman
took one in another room, leaving the room he had
occupied heretofore for the consul. As he was
saying good-night, Albert suggested that he had
not yet told them how he came to be on a deserted
island; but Stedman only laughed and said that
that was a long story, and that he would tell him
all about it in the morning. So Albert went off
to bed without waiting for the consul to return,
and fell asleep, wondering at the strangeness of
his new life, and assuring himself that if the rain
only kept up, he would have his novel finished in
a month.

The sun was shining brightly when he awoke,
and the palm-trees outside were nodding gracefully
in a warm breeze. From the court came the odor
of strange flowers, and from the window he could
see the ocean brilliantly blue, and with the sun col-
oring the spray that beat against the coral reefs
on the shore.

"Well, the consul can't complain of this," he
said, with a laugh of satisfaction; and pulling on
a bath-robe, he stepped into the next room to
awaken Captain Travis. But the room was quite

empty, and the bed undisturbed. The consul's trunk remained just where it had been placed near the door, and on it lay a large sheet of foolscap, with writing on it, and addressed at the top to Albert Gordon. The handwriting was the consul's. Albert picked it up and read it with much anxiety. It began abruptly—

"The fishermen who brought us to this forsaken spot tell me that it rains here six months in the year, and that this is the first month. I came here to serve my country, for which I fought and bled, but I did not come here to die of rheumatism and pneumonia. I can serve my country better by staying alive; and whether it rains or not, I don't like it. I have been grossly deceived, and I am going back. Indeed, by the time you get this, I will be on my return trip, as I intend leaving with the men who brought us here as soon as they can get the sail up. My cousin, Senator Rainsford, can fix it all right with the President, and can have me recalled in proper form after I get back. But of course it would not do for me to leave my post with no one to take my place, and no one could be more ably fitted to do so than yourself; so I feel no compunctions at leaving you behind. I hereby, therefore, accordingly appoint you my substitute with full power to act, to collect all fees, sign all papers, and attend to all matters pertaining to your office as American consul, and I trust you will worthily uphold the name of that country and government which it has always been my pleasure and duty to serve.

"Your sincere friend and superior officer,

"Leonard T. Travis.

"P. S. I did not care to disturb you by moving my trunk, so I left it, and you can make what use you please of whatever it contains, as I shall not want tropical garments where I am going. What you will need most, I think, is a waterproof and umbrella.

"P. S. Look out for that young man Stedman. He is too inventive. I hope you will like your high office; but as for myself, I am satisfied with little old New York. Opeki is just a bit too far from civilization to suit me."

Albert held the letter before him and read it over again before he moved. Then he jumped to the window. The boat was gone, and there was not a sign of it on the horizon.

"The miserable old hypocrite!" he cried, half angry and half laughing. "If he thinks I am going to stay here alone he is very greatly mistaken.

And yet, why not?" he asked. He stopped soliloquizing and looked around him, thinking rapidly. As he stood there, Stedman came in from the other room, fresh and smiling from his morning's bath.

"Good-morning," he said, "where's the consul?"

"The consul," said Albert, gravely, "is before you. In me you see the American consul to Opeki.

"Captain Travis," Albert explained, "has returned to the United States. I suppose he feels that he can best serve his country by remaining on the spot. In case of another war, now, for instance, he would be there to save it again."

"And what are you going to do?" asked Stedman, anxiously. "You will not run away too, will you?"

Albert said that he intended to remain where he was and perform his consular duties, to appoint him his secretary, and to elevate the United States in the opinion of the Opekians above all other nations.

"They may not think much of the United States in England," he said; "but we are going to teach the people of Opeki that America is first on the map and that there is no second."

"I'm sure it's very good of you to make me your

secretary," said Stedman, with some pride. "I hope I won't make any mistakes. What are the duties of a consul's secretary?"

"That," said Albert, "I do not know. But you are rather good at inventing, so you can invent a few. That should be your first duty and you should attend to it at once. I will have trouble enough finding work for myself. Your salary is five hundred dollars a year; and now," he continued, briskly, "we want to prepare for this reception. We can tell the King that Travis was just a guard of honor for the trip, and that I have sent him back to tell the President of my safe arrival. That will keep the President from getting anxious. There is nothing," continued Albert, "like a uniform to impress people who live in the tropics, and Travis, it so happens, has two in his trunk. He intended to wear them on State occasions, and as I inherit the trunk and all that is in it, I intend to wear one of the uniforms, and you can have the other. But I have first choice, because I am consul."

Captain Travis's consular outfit consisted of one full dress and one undress United States uniform. Albert put on the dress-coat over a pair of white flannel trousers, and looked remarkably brave and handsome. Stedman, who was only eighteen and quite thin, did not appear so well, until Albert suggested his padding out his chest and shoulders with towels. This made him rather warm, but helped his general appearance.

"The two Bradleys must dress up, too," said Albert. "I think they ought to act as a guard of honor, don't you? The only things I have are blazers and jerseys; but it doesn't much matter what they wear, as long as they dress alike."

He accordingly called in the two Bradleys, and gave them each a pair of the captain's rejected white duck trousers, and a blue jersey apiece, with a big white Y on it.

"The students of Yale gave me that," he said to the younger Bradley, "in which to play football, and a great man gave me the other. His name is Walter Camp; and if you rip or soil that jersey, I'll send you back to England in irons; so be careful."

Stedman gazed at his companions in their different costumes, doubtfully. "It reminds me," he said, "of private theatricals. Of the time our church choir played 'Pinafore.'"

"Yes," assented Albert; "but I don't think we look quite gay enough. I tell you what we need, —medals. You never saw a diplomat without a lot of decorations and medals."

Made Himself King

"Well, I can fix that," Stedman said. "I've got a trunkful. I used to be the fastest bicycle-rider in Connecticut, and I've got all my prizes with me."

Albert said doubtfully that that wasn't exactly the sort of medal he meant.

"Perhaps not," returned Stedman, as he began fumbling in his trunk; "but the King won't know the difference. He couldn't tell a cross of the Legion of Honor from a medal for the tug of war."

So the bicycle medals, of which Stedman seemed to have an innumerable quantity, were strung in profusion over Albert's uniform, and in a lesser quantity over Stedman's; while a handful of leaden ones, those sold on the streets for the Constitutional Centennial, with which Albert had provided himself, were wrapped up in a red silk handkerchief for presentation to the King; with them Albert placed a number of brass rods and brass chains, much to Stedman's delighted approval.

"That is a very good idea," he said. "Democratic simplicity is the right thing at home, of course; but when you go abroad and mix with crowned heads, you want to show them that you know what's what."

"Well," said Albert, gravely, "I sincerely hope

this crowned head don't know what's what. If he reads 'Connecticut Agricultural State Fair. One mile bicycle race. First Prize,' on this badge, when we are trying to make him believe it's a war medal, it may hurt his feelings."

Bradley, Jr., went ahead to announce the approach of the American embassy, which he did with so much manner that the King deferred the audience a half-hour, in order that he might better prepare to receive his visitors. When the audience did take place, it attracted the entire population to the green spot in front of the King's palace, and their delight and excitement over the appearance of the visitors was sincere and hearty. The King was too polite to appear much surprised, but he showed his delight over his presents as simply and openly as a child. Thrice he insisted on embracing Albert, and kissing him three times on the forehead, which, Stedman assured him in a side-whisper, was a great honor; an honor which was not extended to the secretary, although he was given a necklace of animals' claws instead, with which he was better satisfied.

After this reception, the embassy marched back to the consul's office, surrounded by an immense number of the natives, some of whom ran ahead and looked back at them, and crowded so close that the two Bradleys had to poke at those nearest with their guns. The crowd remained outside the office even after the procession of four had disappeared, and cheered. This suggested to Gordon that this would be a good time to make a speech, which he accordingly did, Stedman translating it, sentence by sentence. At the conclusion of this effort, Albert distributed a number of brass rings among the married men present, which they placed on whichever finger fitted best, and departed delighted.

Albert had wished to give the rings to the married women, but Stedman pointed out to him that it would be much cheaper to give them to the married men; for while one woman could only have one husband, one man could have at least six wives.

"And now, Stedman," said Albert, after the mob had gone, "tell me what you are doing on this island."

"It's a very simple story," Stedman said. "I am the representative, or agent, or operator, for the Yokohama Cable Company. The Yokohama Cable Company is a company organized in San Francisco, for the purpose of laying a cable to Yokohama. It is a stock company; and though it started out very well, the stock has fallen very low. Between ourselves, it is not worth over three or four cents. When the officers of the company found out that no one would buy their stock, and that no one believed in them or their scheme, they laid a cable to Octavia, and extended it on to this island. Then they said they had run out of ready money, and would wait until they got more before laying their cable any farther. I do not think they ever will lay it any farther, but that is none of my business. My business is to answer cable messages from San Francisco, so that the people who visit the home office can see that at least a part of the cable is working. That sometimes impresses them, and they buy stock. There is another chap over in Octavia, who relays all my messages and all my replies to those messages that come to me through him from San Francisco. They never send a message unless they have brought someone to the office whom they want to impress, and who, they think, has money to invest in the Y. C. C. stock, and so we never go near the wire, except at three o'clock every afternoon. And then generally only to say 'How are you?' or 'It's raining,' or something like that. I've been saying 'It's raining,' now for the last three months, but to-day I will say that the new consul has arrived. That will be a pleasant surprise for the chap in Octavia, for he must be tired hearing about the weather. He

generally answers, 'Here too,' or 'So you said,' or
something like that. I don't know what he says
to the home office. He's brighter than I am, and
that's why they put him between the two ends.
He can see that the messages are transmitted more
fully and more correctly, in a way to please possible subscribers."

"Sort of copy editor," suggested Albert.

"Yes, something of that sort, I fancy," said
Stedman.

They walked down to the little shed on the
shore, where the Y. C. C. office was placed, at
three that day, and Albert watched Stedman send
off his message with much interest. The "chap at
Octavia," on being informed that the American
consul had arrived at Opeki, inquired, somewhat
disrespectfully, "Is it a life sentence?"

"What does he mean by that?" asked Albert.

"I suppose," said his secretary, doubtfully,
"that he thinks it a sort of a punishment to be
sent to Opeki. I hope you won't grow to think
so."

"Opeki is all very well," said Gordon, "or it
will be when we get things going our way."

As they walked back to the office, Albert noticed
a brass cannon, perched on a rock at the entrance
to the harbor. This had been put there by the last

consul, but it had not been fired for many years. Albert immediately ordered the two Bradleys to get it in order, and to rig up a flag-pole beside it, for one of his American flags, which they were to salute every night when they lowered it at sundown.

"And when we are not using it," he said, "the King can borrow it to celebrate with, if he doesn't impose on us too often. The royal salute ought to be twenty-one guns, I think; but that would use up too much powder, so he will have to content himself with two."

"Did you notice," asked Stedman, that night, as they sat on the veranda of the consul's house, in the moonlight, "how the people bowed to us as we passed?"

"Yes," Albert said he had noticed it. "Why?"

"Well, they never saluted me," replied Stedman. "That sign of respect is due to the show we made at the reception."

"It is due to us, in any event," said the consul, severely. "I tell you, my secretary, that we, as the representatives of the United States Government, must be properly honored on this island. We must become a power. And we must do so without getting into trouble with the King. We must make them honor him, too, and then as we push him up, we will push ourselves up at the same time."

"They don't think much of consuls in Opeki," said Stedman, doubtfully. "You see the last one was a pretty poor sort. He brought the office into disrepute, and it wasn't really until I came and told them what a fine country the United States was, that they had any opinion of it at all. Now we must change all that."

"That is just what we will do," said Albert. "We will transform Opeki into a powerful and beautiful city. We will make these people work. They must put up a palace for the King, and lay out streets, and build wharves, and drain the town properly, and light it. I haven't seen this patent lighting apparatus of yours, but you had better get to work at it at once, and I'll persuade the King to appoint you commissioner of highways and gas, with authority to make his people toil. And I," he cried, in free enthusiasm, "will organize a navy and a standing army. Only," he added, with a relapse of interest, "there isn't anybody to fight."

"There isn't?" said Stedman, grimly, with a scornful smile. "You just go hunt up old Messenwah and the Hillmen with your standing army once and you'll get all the fighting you want."

"The Hillmen?" said Albert.

"The Hillmen are the natives that live up there in the hills," Stedman said, nodding his head toward the three high mountains at the other end of the island, that stood out blackly against the purple, moonlit sky. "There are nearly as many of them as there are Opekians, and they hunt and fight for a living and for the pleasure of it. They have an old rascal named Messenwah for a king, and they come down here about once every three months, and tear things up."

Albert sprang to his feet.

"Oh, they do, do they?" he said, staring up at the mountain-tops. "They come down here and tear up things, do they? Well, I think we'll stop that, I think we'll stop that! I don't care how many there are. I'll get the two Bradleys to tell me all they know about drilling, to-morrow morning, and we'll drill these Opekians, and have sham battles, and attacks, and repulses, until I make a lot of wild, howling Zulus out of them. And when the Hillmen come down to pay their quarterly visit, they'll go back again on a run. At least some of them will," he added, ferociously. "Some of them will stay right here."

"Dear me, dear me!" said Stedman, with awe; "you are a born fighter, aren't you?"

"Well, you wait and see," said Gordon; "maybe I am. I haven't studied tactics of war and the history of battles, so that I might be a great war-correspondent, without learning something. And there is only one king on this island, and that is old Ollypybus himself. And I'll go over and have a talk with him about it to-morrow."

Young Stedman walked up and down the length of the veranda, in and out of the moonlight, with his hands in his pockets, and his head on his chest. "You have me all stirred up, Gordon," he said; "you seem so confident and bold, and you're not so much older than I am, either."

"My training has been different; that's all," said the reporter.

"Yes," Stedman said, bitterly. "I have been sitting in an office ever since I left school, sending news over a wire or a cable, and you have been out in the world, gathering it."

"And now," said Gordon, smiling, and putting his arm around the other boy's shoulders, "we are going to make news ourselves."

"There is one thing I want to say to you before you turn in," said Stedman. "Before you suggest all these improvements on Ollypybus, you must remember that he has ruled absolutely here for twenty years, and that he does not think much of consuls. He has only seen your predecessor and yourself. He likes you because you appeared with such dignity, and because of the presents; but if I were you, I wouldn't suggest these improvements as coming from yourself."

"I don't understand," said Gordon; "who could they come from?"

"Well," said Stedman, "if you will allow me to advise—and you see I know these people pretty well—I would have all these suggestions come from the President direct."

"The President!" exclaimed Gordon; "but how? What does the President know or care about Opeki? and it would take so long—oh, I see, the cable. Is that what you have been doing?" he asked.

"Well, only once," said Stedman, guiltily; "that was when he wanted to turn me out of the consul's office, and I had a cable that very afternoon, from the President, ordering me to stay where I was. Ollypybus doesn't understand the cable, of course, but he knows that it sends messages; and sometimes I pretend to send messages for him to the President; but he began asking me to tell the President to come and pay him a visit, and I had to stop it."

"I'm glad you told me," said Gordon. "The President shall begin to cable to-morrow. He will need an extra appropriation from Congress to pay for his private cablegrams alone."

Made Himself King

"And there's another thing," said Stedman. "In all your plans, you've arranged for the people's improvement, but not for their amusement; and they are a peaceful, jolly, simple sort of people, and we must please them."

"Have they no games or amusements of their own?" asked Gordon.

"Well, not what we would call games."

"Very well, then, I'll teach them base-ball. Foot-ball would be too warm. But that plaza in front of the King's bungalow, where his palace is going to be, is just the place for a diamond. On the whole, though," added the consul, after a moment's reflection, "you'd better attend to that yourself. I don't think it becomes my dignity as American consul to take off my coat and give lessons to young Opekians in sliding to bases; do you? No; I think you'd better do that. The Bradleys will help you, and you had better begin to-morrow. You have been wanting to know what a secretary of legation's duties are, and now you know. It's to organize base-ball nines. And after you get yours ready," he added, as he turned into his room for the night, "I'll train one that will sweep yours off the face of the island. For *this* American consul can pitch three curves."

The best laid plans of men go far astray, some-

times, and the great and beautiful city that was to
rise on the coast of Opeki was not built in a day.
Nor was it ever built. For before the Bradleys
could mark out the foul-lines for the base-ball
field on the plaza, or teach their standing army the
goose step, or lay bamboo pipes for the water-
mains, or clear away the cactus for the extension
of the King's palace, the Hillmen paid Opeki their
quarterly visit.

Albert had called on the King the next morning,
with Stedman as his interpreter, as he had said he
would, and, with maps and sketches, had shown
his Majesty what he proposed to do toward improving Opeki and ennobling her king, and
when the King saw Albert's free-hand sketches of
wharves with tall ships lying at anchor, and rows
of Opekian warriors with the Bradleys at their
head, and the design for his new palace, and a royal
sedan chair, he believed that these things were already his, and not still only on paper, and he appointed Albert his Minister of War, Stedman his
Minister of Home Affairs, and selected two of his
wisest and oldest subjects to serve them as joint
advisers. His enthusiasm was even greater than
Gordon's, because he did not appreciate the difficulties. He thought Gordon a semi-god, a worker of
miracles, and urged the putting up of a monument

to him at once in the public plaza, to which Albert
objected, on the ground that it would be too sug-
gestive of an idol; and to which Stedman also objected, but for the less unselfish reason that it would
"be in the way of the pitcher's box."

They were feverishly discussing all these great
changes, and Stedman was translating as rapidly as
he could translate, the speeches of four different
men—for the two counsellors had been called in
—all of whom wanted to speak at once when there
came from outside a great shout, and the screams
of women, and the clashing of iron, and the patter-
ing footsteps of men running.

As they looked at one another in startled surprise, a native ran into the room, followed by
Bradley, Jr., and threw himself down before the
King. While he talked, beating his hands and
bowing before Ollypybus, Bradley, Jr., pulled his
forelock to the consul, and told how this man lived
on the far outskirts of the village; how he had
been captured while out hunting, by a number of
the Hillmen; and how he had escaped to tell the
people that their old enemies were on the war-path
again, and rapidly approaching the village.

Outside, the women were gathering in the plaza,
with the children about them, and the men were
running from hut to hut, warning their fellows,

and arming themselves with spears and swords, and the native bows and arrows.

"They might have waited until we had that army trained," said Gordon, in a tone of the keenest displeasure. "Tell me, quick, what do they generally do when they come?"

"Steal all the cattle and goats, and a woman or two, and set fire to the huts in the outskirts," replied Stedman.

"Well, we must stop them," said Gordon, jumping up. "We must take out a flag of truce and treat with them. They must be kept off until I have my army in working order. It is most inconvenient. If they had only waited two months, now, or six weeks even, we could have done something; but now we must make peace. Tell the King we are going out to fix things with them, and tell him to keep off his warriors until he learns whether we succeed or fail."

"But, Gordon!" gasped Stedman. "Albert! You don't understand. Why, man, this isn't a street-fight or a cane-rush. They'll stick you full of spears, dance on your body, and eat you, maybe. A flag of truce!—you're talking nonsense. What do they know of a flag of truce?"

"You're talking nonsense, too," said Albert, "and you're talking to your superior officer. If

you are not with me in this, go back to your cable,
and tell the man in Octavia that it's a warm day,
and that the sun is shining; but if you've any spirit
in you—and I think you have—run to the office
and get my Winchester rifles, and the two shot-
guns, and my revolvers, and my uniform, and a
lot of brass things for presents, and run all the
way there and back. And make time. Play you're
riding a bicycle at the Agricultural Fair."

Stedman did not hear this last, for he was already off and away, pushing through the crowd,
and calling on Bradley, Sr., to follow him. Bradley, Jr., looked at Gordon with eyes that snapped,
like a dog that is waiting for his master to throw
a stone.

"I can fire a Winchester, sir," he said. "Old
Tom can't. He's no good at long range 'cept with
a big gun, sir. Don't give him the Winchester.
Give it to me, please, sir."

Albert met Stedman in the plaza, and pulled off
his blazer, and put on Captain Travis's—now his
—uniform coat, and his white pith helmet.

"Now, Jack," he said, "get up there and tell
these people that we are going out to make peace
with these Hillmen, or bring them back prisoners
of war. Tell them we are the preservers of their
homes and wives and children; and you, Bradley,

take these presents, and young Bradley, keep close to me, and carry this rifle."

Stedman's speech was hot and wild enough to suit a critical and feverish audience before a barricade in Paris. And when he was through, Gordon and Bradley punctuated his oration by firing off the two Winchester rifles in the air, at which the people jumped and fell on their knees, and prayed to their several gods. The fighting men of the village followed the four white men to the outskirts, and took up their stand there as Stedman told them to do, and the four walked on over the roughly hewn road, to meet the enemy.

Gordon walked with Bradley, Jr., in advance. Stedman and old Tom Bradley followed close behind, with the two shot-guns, and the presents in a basket.

"Are these Hillmen used to guns?" asked Gordon. Stedman said no, they were not.

"This shot-gun of mine is the only one on the island," he explained, "and we never came near enough them before to do anything with it. It only carries a hundred yards. The Opekians never make any show of resistance. They are quite content if the Hillmen satisfy themselves with the outlying huts, as long as they leave them and the town alone; so they seldom come to close quarters."

Made Himself King

The four men walked on for half an hour or so in silence, peering eagerly on every side; but it was not until they had left the woods and marched out into the level stretch of grassy country that they came upon the enemy. The Hillmen were about forty in number, and were as savage and ugly-looking giants as any in a picture-book. They had captured a dozen cows and goats, and were driving them on before them, as they advanced farther upon the village. When they saw the four men, they gave a mixed chorus of cries and yells, and some of them stopped, and others ran forward, shaking their spears, and shooting their broad arrows into the ground before them. A tall, gray-bearded, muscular old man, with a skirt of feathers about him, and necklaces of bones and animals' claws around his bare chest, ran in front of them, and seemed to be trying to make them approach more slowly.

"Is that Messenwah?" asked Gordon.

"Yes," said Stedman; "he is trying to keep them back. I don't believe he ever saw a white man before."

"Stedman," said Albert, speaking quickly, "give your gun to Bradley, and go forward with your arms in the air, and waving your handkerchief, and tell them in their language that the King is com-

ing. If they go at you, Bradley and I will kill ⌐
goat or two, to show them what we can do with
the rifles; and if that don't stop them, we will shoot
at their legs; and if that don't stop them—I guess
you'd better come back, and we'll all run."

Stedman looked at Albert, and Albert looked
at Stedman, and neither of them winced or flinched.

"Is this another of my secretary's duties?" asked
the younger boy.

"Yes," said the consul; "but a resignation is always in order. You needn't go if you don't like
it. You see, you know the language and I don't,
but I know how to shoot, and you don't."

"That's perfectly satisfactory," said Stedman,
handing his gun to old Bradley. "I only wanted
to know why I was to be sacrificed instead of one
of the Bradleys. It's because I know the language.
Bradley, Sr., you see the evil results of a higher
education. Wish me luck, please," he said, "and
for goodness' sake," he added impressively, "don't
waste much time shooting goats."

The Hillmen had stopped about two hundred
yards off, and were drawn up in two lines, shouting,
and dancing, and hurling taunting remarks at their
few adversaries. The stolen cattle were bunched
together back of the King. As Stedman walked
steadily forward with his handkerchief fluttering,

and howling out something in their own tongue, they stopped and listened. As he advanced, his three companions followed him at about fifty yards in the rear. He was one hundred and fifty yards from the Hillmen before they made out what he said, and then one of the young braves, resenting it as an insult to his chief, shot an arrow at him. Stedman dodged the arrow and stood his ground without even taking a step backward, only turning slightly to put his hands to his mouth, and to shout something which sounded to his companions like, "About time to begin on the goats." But the instant the young man had fired, King Messenwah swung his club and knocked him down, and none of the others moved. Then Messenwah advanced before his men to meet Stedman, and on Stedman's opening and shutting his hands to show that he was unarmed, the King threw down his club and spears, and came forward as empty-handed as himself.

"Ah," gasped Bradley, Jr., with his finger trembling on his lever, "let me take a shot at him now." Gordon struck the man's gun up, and walked forward in all the glory of his gold and blue uniform; for both he and Stedman saw now that Messenwah was more impressed by their appearance, and in the fact that they were white men, than with any threats of immediate war. So when he saluted Gordon haughtily, that young man gave him a haughty nod in return, and bade Stedman tell the King that he would permit him to sit down. The King did not quite appear to like this, but he sat down, nevertheless, and nodded his head gravely.

"Now tell him," said Gordon, "that I come from the ruler of the greatest nation on earth, and that I recognize Ollypybus as the only King of this island, and that I come to this little three-penny King with either peace and presents, or bullets and war."

"Have I got to tell him he's a little three-penny King?" said Stedman, plaintively.

"No; you needn't give a literal translation; it can be as free as you please."

"Thanks," said the secretary, humbly.

"And tell him," continued Gordon, "that we will give presents to him and his warriors if he keeps away from Ollypybus, and agrees to keep away always. If he won't do that, try to get him to agree to stay away for three months at least, and by that time we can get word to San Francisco, and have a dozen muskets over here in two months; and when our time of probation is up, and he and his merry men come dancing down the hillside, we will blow them up as high as his mountains. But

About Time to Begin on the Goats.

you needn't tell him that, either. And if he is proud and haughty, and would rather fight, ask him to restrain himself until we show what we can do with our weapons at two hundred yards."

Stedman seated himself in the long grass in front of the King, and with many revolving gestures of his arms, and much pointing at Gordon, and profound nods and bows, retold what Gordon had dictated. When he had finished, the King looked at the bundle of presents, and at the guns, of which Stedman had given a very wonderful account, but answered nothing.

"I guess," said Stedman, with a sigh, "that we will have to give him a little practical demonstration to help matters. I am sorry, but I think one of those goats has got to die. It's like vivisection. The lower order of animals have to suffer for the good of the higher."

"Oh," said Bradley, Jr., cheerfully, "I'd just as soon shoot one of those niggers as one of the goats."

So Stedman bade the King tell his men to drive a goat toward them, and the King did so, and one of the men struck one of the goats with his spear, and it ran clumsily across the plain.

"Take your time, Bradley," said Gordon. "Aim low, and if you hit it, you can have it for supper."

"And if you miss it," said Stedman, gloomily, "Messenwah may have us for supper."

The Hillmen had seated themselves a hundred yards off, while the leaders were debating, and they now rose curiously and watched Bradley, as he sank upon one knee, and covered the goat with his rifle. When it was about one hundred and fifty yards off he fired, and the goat fell over dead.

And then all the Hillmen, with the King himself, broke away on a run, toward the dead animal, with much shouting. The King came back alone, leaving his people standing about and examining the goat. He was much excited, and talked and gesticulated violently.

"He says—" said Stedman; "he says——"

"What? yes, go on."

"He says—goodness me!—what do you think he says?"

"Well, what does he say?" cried Gordon, in great excitement. "Don't keep it all to yourself."

"He says," said Stedman, "that we are deceived; that he is no longer King of the Island of Opeki; that he is in great fear of us, and that he has got himself into no end of trouble. He says he sees that we are indeed mighty men, that to us he is as helpless as the wild boar before the javelin of the hunter."

Made Himself King

"Well, he's right," said Gordon. "Go on."

"But that which we ask is no longer his to give. He has sold his kingship and his right to this island to another king, who came to him two days ago in a great canoe, and who made noises as we do—with guns, I suppose he means—and to whom he sold the island for a watch that he has in a bag around his neck. And that he signed a paper, and made marks on a piece of bark, to show that he gave up the island freely and forever."

"What does he mean?" said Gordon. "How can he give up the island? Ollypybus is the king of half of it, anyway, and he knows it."

"That's just it," said Stedman. "That's what frightens him. He said he didn't care about Ollypybus, and didn't count him in when he made the treaty, because he is such a peaceful chap that he knew he could thrash him into doing anything he wanted him to do. And now that you have turned up and taken Ollypybus's part, he wishes he hadn't sold the island, and wishes to know if you are angry."

"Angry? of course I'm angry," said Gordon, glaring as grimly at the frightened monarch as he thought was safe. "Who wouldn't be angry? Who do you think these people were who made

185

a fool of him, Stedman? Ask him to let us see this watch."

Stedman did so, and the King fumbled among his necklaces until he had brought out a leather bag tied round his neck with a cord, and containing a plain stem-winding silver watch marked on the inside "Munich."

"That doesn't tell anything," said Gordon. "But it's plain enough. Some foreign ship of war has settled on this place as a coaling-station, or has annexed it for colonization, and they've sent a boat ashore, and they've made a treaty with this old chap, and forced him to sell his birthright for a mess of porridge. Now, that's just like those monarchical pirates, imposing upon a poor old black."

Old Bradley looked at him impudently.

"Not at all," said Gordon; "it's quite different with us; we don't want to rob him or Ollypybus, or to annex their land. All we want to do is to improve it, and have the fun of running it for them and meddling in their affairs of state. Well, Stedman," he said, "what shall we do?"

Stedman said that the best and only thing to do was to threaten to take the watch away from Messenwah, but to give him a revolver instead, which would make a friend of him for life, and to keep him supplied with cartridges only as long as he behaved himself, and then to make him understand that, as Ollypybus had not given his consent to the loss of the island, Messenwah's agreement, or treaty, or whatever it was, did not stand, and that he had better come down the next day, early in the morning, and join in a general consultation. This was done, and Messenwah agreed willingly to their proposition, and was given his revolver and shown how to shoot it, while the other presents were distributed among the other men, who were as happy over them as girls with a full dance-card.

"And now, to-morrow," said Stedman, "understand, you are all to come down unarmed, and sign a treaty with great Ollypybus, in which he will agree to keep to one-half of the island if you keep to yours, and there must be no more wars or goat-stealing, or this gentleman on my right and I will come up and put holes in you just as the gentleman on the left did with the goat."

Messenwah and his warriors promised to come early, and saluted reverently as Gordon and his three companions walked up together very proudly and stiffly.

"Do you know how I feel?" said Gordon.

"How?" asked Stedman.

"I feel as I used to do in the city, when the

boys in the street were throwing snowballs, and I had to go by with a high hat on my head and pretend not to know they were behind me. I always felt a cold chill down my spinal column, and I could feel that snowball, whether it came or not, right in the small of my back. And I can feel one of those men pulling his bow now, and the arrow sticking out of my right shoulder."

"Oh, no, you can't," said Stedman. "They are too much afraid of those rifles. But I do feel sorry for any of those warriors whom old man Messenwah doesn't like, now that he has that revolver. He isn't the sort to practise on goats."

There was great rejoicing when Stedman and Gordon told their story to the King, and the people learned that they were not to have their huts burned and their cattle stolen. The armed Opekians formed a guard around the ambassadors and escorted them to their homes with cheers and shouts, and the women ran at their side and tried to kiss Gordon's hand.

"I'm sorry I can't speak the language, Stedman," said Gordon, "or I would tell them what a brave man you are. You are too modest to do it yourself, even if I dictated something for you to say. As for me," he said, pulling off his uniform, "I am thoroughly disgusted and disappointed. It never occurred to me until it was all over that this was my chance to be a war-correspondent. It wouldn't have been much of a war, but then I would have been the only one on the spot, and that counts for a great deal. Still, my time may come."

"We have a great deal on hand for to-morrow," said Gordon that evening, "and we had better turn in early."

And so the people were still singing and rejoicing down in the village when the two conspirators for the peace of the country went to sleep for the night. It seemed to Gordon as though he had hardly turned his pillow twice to get the coolest side when someone touched him, and he saw, by the light of the dozen glow-worms in the tumbler by his bedside, a tall figure at its foot.

"It's me—Bradley," said the figure.

"Yes," said Gordon, with the haste of a man to show that sleep has no hold on him; "exactly; what is it?"

"There is a ship of war in the harbor," Bradley answered in a whisper. "I heard her anchor chains rattle when she came to, and that woke me. I could hear that if I were dead. And then I made sure by her lights; she's a great boat, sir, and I can know she's a ship of war by the challenging when they change the watch. I thought you'd like to know, sir."

Gordon sat up and clutched his knees with his hands. "Yes, of course," he said; "you are quite right. Still, I don't see what there is to do."

He did not wish to show too much youthful interest, but though fresh from civilization, he had learned how far from it he was, and he was curious to see this sign of it that had come so much more quickly than he had anticipated.

"Wake Mr. Stedman, will you?" said he, "and we will go and take a look at her."

"You can see nothing but the lights," said Bradley, as he left the room; "it's a black night, sir."

Stedman was not new from the sight of men and ships of war, and came in half dressed and eager.

"Do you suppose it's the big canoe Messenwah spoke of?" he said.

"I thought of that," said Gordon.

The three men fumbled their way down the road to the plaza, and saw, as soon as they turned into it, the great outlines and the brilliant lights of an immense vessel, still more immense in the darkness, and glowing like a strange monster of the sea, with just a suggestion here and there, where the lights spread, of her cabins and bridges. As they stood on the shore, shivering in the cool night-wind, they heard the bells strike over the water.

"It's two o'clock," said Bradley, counting.

"Well, we can do nothing, and they cannot mean to do much to-night," Albert said. "We had better get some more sleep, and, Bradley, you keep watch and tell us as soon as day breaks."

"Aye, aye, sir," said the sailor.

"If that's the man-of-war that made the treaty with Messenwah, and Messenwah turns up to-morrow, it looks as if our day would be pretty well filled up," said Albert, as they felt their way back to the darkness.

"What do you intend to do?" asked his secretary, with a voice of some concern.

"I don't know," Albert answered gravely, from the blackness of the night. "It looks as if we were getting ahead just a little too fast, doesn't it? Well," he added, as they reached the house, "let's try to keep in step with the procession, even if we can't be drum-majors and walk in front of it." And with this cheering tone of confidence in their ears, the two diplomats went soundly asleep again.

The light of the rising sun filled the room, and the parrots were chattering outside, when Bradley woke him again.

"They are sending a boat ashore, sir," he said,

excitedly, and filled with the importance of the occasion. "She's a German man-of-war, and one of the new model. A beautiful boat, sir; for her lines were laid in Glasgow, and I can tell that, no matter what flag she flies. You had best be moving to meet them: the village isn't awake yet."

Albert took a cold bath and dressed leisurely; then he made Bradley, Jr., who had slept through it all, get up breakfast, and the two young men ate it and drank their coffee comfortably and with an air of confidence that deceived their servants, if it did not deceive themselves. But when they came down the path, smoking and swinging their sticks, and turned into the plaza, their composure left them like a mask, and they stopped where they stood. The plaza was enclosed by the natives gathered in whispering groups, and depressed by fear and wonder. On one side were crowded all the Messenwah warriors, unarmed, and as silent and disturbed as the Opekians. In the middle of the plaza some twenty sailors were busy rearing and bracing a tall flag-staff that they had shaped from a royal palm, and they did this as unconcernedly and as contemptuously, and with as much indifference to the strange groups on either side of them, as though they were working on a barren coast, with nothing but the startled sea-gulls about them. As Albert and Stedman came upon the scene, the flag-pole was in place, and the halyards hung from it with a little bundle of bunting at the end of one of them.

"We must find the King at once," said Gordon. He was terribly excited and angry. "It is easy enough to see what this means. They are going through the form of annexing this island to the other lands of the German Government. They are robbing old Ollypybus of what is his. They have not even given him a silver watch for it."

The King was in his bungalow, facing the plaza. Messenwah was with him, and an equal number of each of their councils. The common danger had made them lie down together in peace; but they gave a murmur of relief as Gordon strode into the room with no ceremony, and greeted them with a curt wave of the hand.

"Now then, Stedman, be quick," he said. "Explain to them what this means; tell them that I will protect them; that I am anxious to see that Ollypybus is not cheated; that we will do all we can for them."

Outside, on the shore, a second boat's crew had landed a group of officers and a file of marines. They walked in all the dignity of full dress across the plaza to the flag-pole, and formed in line on the three sides of it, with the marines facing the sea. The officers, from the captain with a prayer-book in his hand, to the youngest middy, were as indifferent to the frightened natives about them as the other men had been. The natives, awed and afraid, crouched back among their huts, the marines and the sailors kept their eyes front, and the German captain opened his prayer-book. The debate in the bungalow was over.

"If you only had your uniform, sir," said Bradley, Sr., miserably.

"This is a little bit too serious for uniforms and bicycle medals," said Gordon. "And these men are used to gold lace."

He pushed his way through the natives, and stepped confidently across the plaza. The youngest middy saw him coming, and nudged the one next him with his elbow, and he nudged the next, but none of the officers moved, because the captain had begun to read.

"One minute, please," called Gordon.

He stepped out into the hollow square formed by the marines, and raised his helmet to the captain.

"Do you speak English or French?" Gordon said in French; "I do not understand German."

Made Himself King

The captain lowered the book in his hands and gazed reflectively at Gordon through his spectacles, and made no reply.

"If I understand this," said the younger man, trying to be very impressive and polite, "you are laying claim to this land, in behalf of the German Government."

The captain continued to observe him thoughtfully, and then said, "That iss so," and then asked, "Who are you?"

"I represent the King of this island, Ollypybus, whose people you see around you. I also represent the United States Government, that does not tolerate a foreign power near her coast, since the days of President Monroe and before. The treaty you have made with Messenwah is an absurdity. There is only one king with whom to treat, and he——"

The captain turned to one of his officers and said something, and then, after giving another curious glance at Gordon, raised his book and continued reading, in a deep, unruffled monotone. The officer whispered an order, and two of the marines stepped out of line, and dropping the muzzles of their muskets, pushed Gordon back out of the enclosure, and left him there with his lips white, and trembling all over with indignation. He would

have liked to have rushed back into the lines and
broken the captain's spectacles over his sun-tanned
nose and cheeks, but he was quite sure this would
only result in his getting shot, or in his being made
ridiculous before the natives, which was almost as
bad; so he stood still for a moment, with his blood
choking him, and then turned and walked back to
where the King and Stedman were whispering together. Just as he turned, one of the men pulled
the halyards, the ball of bunting ran up into the
air, bobbed, twitched, and turned, and broke into
the folds of the German flag. At the same moment the marines raised their muskets and fired a
volley, and the officers saluted and the sailors
cheered.

"Do you see that?" cried Stedman, catching
Gordon's humor, to Ollypybus; "that means that
you are no longer king, that strange people are
coming here to take your land, and to turn your
people into servants, and to drive you back into
the mountains. Are you going to submit? are you
going to let that flag stay where it is?"

Messenwah and Ollypybus gazed at one another
with fearful, helpless eyes. "We are afraid,"
Ollypybus cried; "we do not know what we should
do."

"What do they say?"

Made Himself King

"They say they do not know what to do."

"I know what I'd do," cried Gordon. "If I were not an American consul, I'd pull down their old flag, and put a hole in their boat and sink her."

"Well, I'd wait until they get under way before you do either of those things," said Stedman, soothingly. "That captain seems to be a man of much determination of character."

"But I will pull it down," cried Gordon. "I will resign, as Travis did. I am no longer consul. You can be consul if you want to. I promote you. I am going up a step higher. I mean to be king. Tell those two," he ran on, excitedly, "that their only course and only hope is in me; that they must make me ruler of the island until this thing is over; that I will resign again as soon as it is settled, but that someone must act at once, and if they are afraid to, I am not, only they must give me authority to act for them. They must abdicate in my favor."

"Are you in earnest?" gasped Stedman.

"Don't I talk as if I were?" demanded Gordon, wiping the perspiration from his forehead.

"And can I be consul?" said Stedman, cheerfully.

"Of course. Tell them what I propose to do."

Stedman turned and spoke rapidly to the two kings. The people gathered closer to hear.

The two rival monarchs looked at one another in silence for a moment, and then both began to speak at once, their counsellors interrupting them and mumbling their guttural comments with anxious earnestness. It did not take them very long to see that they were all of one mind, and then they both turned to Gordon and dropped on one knee, and placed his hands on their foreheads, and Stedman raised his cap.

"They agree," he explained, for it was but pantomime to Albert. "They salute you as a ruler; they are calling you Tellaman, which means peacemaker. The Peacemaker, that is your title. I hope you will deserve it, but I think they might have chosen a more appropriate one."

"Then I'm really King?" demanded Albert, decidedly, "and I can do what I please? They give me full power. Quick, do they?"

"Yes, but don't do it," begged Stedman, "and just remember I am American consul now, and that is a much superior being to a crowned monarch; you said so yourself."

Albert did not reply to this, but ran across the plaza, followed by the two Bradleys. The boats had gone.

Made Himself King

"Hoist that flag beside the brass cannon," he cried, "and stand ready to salute it when I drop this one."

Bradley, Jr., grasped the halyards of the flag, which he had forgotten to raise and salute in the morning in all the excitement of the arrival of the man-of-war. Bradley, Sr., stood by the brass cannon, blowing gently on his lighted fuse. The Peacemaker took the halyards of the German flag in his two hands, gave a quick, sharp tug, and down came the red, white, and black piece of bunting, and the next moment young Bradley sent the Stars and Stripes up in their place. As it rose, Bradley's brass cannon barked merrily like a little bull-dog, and the Peacemaker cheered.

"Why don't you cheer, Stedman?" he shouted. "Tell those people to cheer for all they are worth. What sort of an American consul are you?"

Stedman raised his arm half-heartedly to give the time, and opened his mouth; but his arm remained fixed and his mouth open, while his eyes stared at the retreating boat of the German man-of-war. In the stern sheets of this boat the stout German captain was struggling unsteadily to his feet; he raised his arm and waved it to someone on the great man-of-war, as though giving an order. The natives looked from Stedman to the boat, and even Gordon stopped in his cheering, and stood motionless, watching. They had not very long to wait. There was a puff of white smoke, and a flash, and then a loud report, and across the water came a great black ball skipping lightly through and over the waves, as easily as a flat stone thrown by a boy. It seemed to come very slowly. At least it came slowly enough for everyone to see that it was coming directly toward the brass cannon. The Bradleys certainly saw this, for they ran as fast as they could, and kept on running. The ball caught the cannon under its mouth and tossed it in the air, knocking the flag-pole into a dozen pieces, and passing on through two of the palm-covered huts.

"Great Heavens, Gordon!" cried Stedman; "they are firing on us."

But Gordon's face was radiant and wild.

"Firing on *us!*" he cried. "On us! Don't you see? Don't you understand? What do *we* amount to? They have fired on the American flag! Don't you see what that means? It means war. A great international war. And I am a war-correspondent at last!" He ran up to Stedman and seized him by the arm so tightly that it hurt.

"By three o'clock," he said, "they will know in the office what has happened. The country will know it to-morrow when the paper is on the street; people will read it all over the world. The Emperor will hear of it at breakfast; the President will cable for further particulars. He will get them. It is the chance of a lifetime, and we are on the spot!"

Stedman did not hear this; he was watching the broadside of the ship to see another puff of white smoke, but there came no such sign. The two row-boats were raised, there was a cloud of black smoke from the funnel, a creaking of chains sounding faintly across the water, and the ship started at half-speed and moved out of the harbor. The Opekians and the Hillmen fell on their knees, or to dancing, as best suited their sense of relief, but Gordon shook his head.

"They are only going to land the marines," he said; "perhaps they are going to the spot they stopped at before, or to take up another position farther out at sea. They will land men and then shell the town, and the land forces will march here and co-operate with the vessel, and everybody will be taken prisoner or killed. We have the centre of the stage, and we are making history."

"I'd rather read it than make it," said Stedman. "You've got us in a senseless, silly position, Gordon, and a mighty unpleasant one. And for no reason that I can see, except to make copy for your paper."

"Tell those people to get their things together," said Gordon, "and march back out of danger into the woods. Tell Ollypybus I am going to fix things all right; I don't know just how yet, but I will, and now come after me as quickly as you can to the cable office. I've got to tell the paper all about it."

It was three o'clock before the "chap at Octavia" answered Stedman's signalling. Then Stedman delivered Gordon's message, and immediately shut off all connection, before the Octavia operator could question him. Gordon dictated his message in this way:—

"Begin with the date line, 'Opeki, June 22.'

"At seven o'clock this morning, the captain and officers of the German man-of-war Kaiser went through the ceremony of annexing this island in the name of the German Emperor, basing their right to do so on an agreement made with a leader of a wandering tribe known as the Hillmen. King Ollypybus, the present monarch of Opeki, delegated his authority, as also did the leader of the Hillmen, to King Tellaman, or the Peacemaker, who tore down the German flag, and raised that of the United States in its place. At the same moment the flag was saluted by the battery. This

Made Himself King

salute, being mistaken for an attack on the Kaiser, was answered by that vessel. Her first shot took immediate effect, completely destroying the entire battery of the Opekians, cutting down the American flag, and destroying the houses of the people——"

"There was only one brass cannon and two huts," expostulated Stedman.

"Well, that was the whole battery, wasn't it?" asked Gordon, "and two huts is plural. I said houses of the people. I couldn't say two houses of the people. Just you send this as you get it. You are not an American consul at the present moment. You are an under-paid agent of a cable company, and you send my stuff as I write it. The American residents have taken refuge in the consulate—that's us," explained Gordon, "and the English residents have sought refuge in the woods—that's the Bradleys. King Tellaman—that's me—declares his intention of fighting against the annexation. The forces of the Opekians are under the command of Captain Thomas Bradley—I guess I might as well make him a colonel—of Colonel Thomas Bradley, of the English army.

"The American consul says—Now, what do you say, Stedman? Hurry up, please," asked Gordon, "and say something good and strong."

"You get me all mixed up," complained Stedman, plaintively. "Which am I now, a cable operator or the American consul?"

"Consul, of course. Say something patriotic and about your determination to protect the interests of your government, and all that." Gordon bit the end of his pencil impatiently, and waited.

"I won't do anything of the sort, Gordon," said Stedman; "you are getting me into an awful lot of trouble, and yourself too. I won't say a word."

"The American consul," read Gordon, as his pencil wriggled across the paper, "refuses to say anything for publication until he has communicated with the authorities at Washington, but from all I can learn he sympathizes entirely with Tellaman. Your correspondent has just returned from an audience with King Tellaman, who asks him to inform the American people that the Monroe doctrine will be sustained as long as he rules this island. I guess that's enough to begin with," said Gordon. "Now send that off quick, and then get away from the instrument before the man in Octavia begins to ask questions. I am going out to precipitate matters."

Gordon found the two kings sitting dejectedly side by side, and gazing grimly upon the disorder of the village, from which the people were taking their leave as quickly as they could get their few belongings piled upon the ox-carts. Gordon walked among them, helping them in every way he could, and tasting, in their subservience and gratitude, the sweets of sovereignty. When Stedman had locked up the cable office and rejoined him, he bade him tell Messenwah to send three of his youngest men and fastest runners back to the hills to watch for the German vessel and see where she was attempting to land her marines.

"This is a tremendous chance for descriptive writing, Stedman," said Gordon, enthusiastically; "all this confusion and excitement, and the people leaving their homes, and all that. It's like the people getting out of Brussels before Waterloo, and then the scene at the foot of the mountains, while they are camping out there, until the Germans leave. I never had a chance like this before."

It was quite dark by six o'clock, and none of the three messengers had as yet returned. Gordon walked up and down the empty plaza and looked now at the horizon for the man-of-war, and again down the road back of the village. But neither the vessel nor the messengers bearing word of her appeared. The night passed without any incident, and in the morning Gordon's impatience became so great that he walked out to where the villagers were in camp and passed on half way up the mountain, but he could see no sign of the man-of-war. He came back more restless than before, and keenly disappointed.

"If something don't happen before three o'clock, Stedman," he said, "our second cablegram will have to consist of glittering generalities and a lengthy interview with King Tellaman, by himself."

Nothing did happen. Ollypybus and Messen-wah began to breathe more freely. They believed the new king had succeeded in frightening the German vessel away forever. But the new king upset their hopes by telling them that the Germans had undoubtedly already landed, and had probably killed the three messengers.

"Now then," he said, with pleased expectation, as Stedman and he seated themselves in the cable office at three o'clock, "open it up and let's find out what sort of an impression we have made."

Stedman's face, as the answer came in to his first message of greeting, was one of strangely marked disapproval.

"What does he say?" demanded Gordon, anxiously.

"He hasn't done anything but swear yet," answered Stedman, grimly.

Made Himself King

"What is he swearing about?"

"He wants to know why I left the cable yesterday. He says he has been trying to call me up for the last twenty-four hours, ever since I sent my message at three o'clock. The home office is jumping mad, and want me discharged. They won't do that, though," he said, in a cheerful aside, "because they haven't paid me my salary for the last eight months. He says—great Scott! this will please you, Gordon—he says that there have been over two hundred queries for matter from papers all over the United States, and from Europe. Your paper beat them on the news, and now the home office is packed with San Francisco reporters, and the telegrams are coming in every minute, and they have been abusing him for not answering them, and he says that I'm a fool. He wants as much as you can send, and all the details. He says all the papers will have to put 'By Yokohama Cable Company' on the top of each message they print, and that that is advertising the company, and is sending the stock up. It rose fifteen points on 'change in San Francisco to-day, and the president and the other officers are buying——"

"Oh, I don't want to hear about their old company," snapped out Gordon, pacing up and down in despair. "What am I to do? that's what I want to know. Here I have the whole country stirred up and begging for news. On their knees for it, and a cable all to myself, and the only man on the spot, and nothing to say. I'd just like to know how long that German idiot intends to wait before he begins shelling this town and killing people. He has put me in a most absurd position."

"Here's a message for you, Gordon," said Stedman, with business-like calm. "Albert Gordon, Correspondent," he read: "Try American consul. First message O. K.; beat the country; can take all you send. Give names of foreign residents massacred, and fuller account blowing up palace. Dodge."

The expression on Gordon's face as this message was slowly read off to him, had changed from one of gratified pride to one of puzzled consternation.

"What's he mean by foreign residents massacred, and blowing up of palace?" asked Stedman, looking over his shoulder anxiously. "Who is Dodge?"

"Dodge is the night editor," said Gordon, nervously. "They must have read my message wrong. You sent just what I gave you, didn't you?" he asked.

"Of course I did," said Stedman, indignantly.

"I didn't say anything about the massacre of

anybody, did I?" asked Gordon. "I hope they are
not improving on my account. What *am* I to do?
This is getting awful. I'll have to go out and kill
a few people myself. Oh, why don't that Dutch
captain begin to do something! What sort of a
fighter does he call himself? He wouldn't shoot
at a school of porpoises. He's not——"

"Here comes a message to Leonard T. Travis,
American consul, Opeki," read Stedman. "It's
raining messages to-day. 'Send full details of
massacre of American citizens by German sailors.'
Secretary of—great Scott!" gasped Stedman, interrupting himself and gazing at his instrument
with horrified fascination — "the Secretary of
State."

"That settles it," roared Gordon, pulling at his
hair and burying his face in his hands. "I have
got to kill some of them now."

"Albert Gordon, Correspondent," read Stedman, impressively, like the voice of Fate. "Is
Colonel Thomas Bradley commanding native
forces at Opeki, Colonel Sir Thomas Kent-Brad-
ley of Crimean war fame? Correspondent London *Times,* San Francisco Press Club."

"Go on, go on!" said Gordon, desperately.
"I'm getting used to it now. Go on!"

"American consul, Opeki," read Stedman.

"Home Secretary desires you to furnish list of names English residents killed during shelling of Opeki by ship of war Kaiser, and estimate of amount property destroyed. Stoughton, British Embassy, Washington."

"Stedman!" cried Gordon, jumping to his feet, "there's a mistake here somewhere. These people cannot all have made my message read like that. Someone has altered it, and now I have got to make these people here live up to that message, whether they like being massacred and blown up or not. Don't answer any of those messages except the one from Dodge; tell him things have quieted down a bit, and that I'll send four thousand words on the flight of the natives from the village, and their encampment at the foot of the mountains, and of the exploring party we have sent out to look for the German vessel; and now I am going out to make something happen."

Gordon said that he would be gone for two hours at least, and as Stedman did not feel capable of receiving any more nerve-stirring messages, he cut off all connection with Octavia by saying, "Good-by for two hours," and running away from the office. He sat down on a rock on the beach, and mopped his face with his handkerchief.

"After a man has taken nothing more exciting

than weather reports from Octavia for a year," he soliloquized, "it's a bit disturbing to have all the crowned heads of Europe and their secretaries calling upon you for details of a massacre that never came off."

At the end of two hours Gordon returned from the consulate with a mass of manuscript in his hand.

"Here's three thousand words," he said, desperately. "I never wrote more and said less in my life. It will make them weep at the office. I had to pretend that they knew all that had happened so far; they apparently do know more than we do, and I have filled it full of prophesies of more trouble ahead, and with interviews with myself and the two ex-Kings. The only news element in it is, that the messengers have returned to report that the German vessel is not in sight, and that there is no news. They think she has gone for good. Suppose she has, Stedman," he groaned, looking at him helplessly, "what *am* I going to do?"

"Well, as for me," said Stedman, "I'm afraid to go near that cable. It's like playing with a live wire. My nervous system won't stand many more such shocks as those they gave us this morning."

Gordon threw himself down dejectedly in a

chair in the office, and Stedman approached his instrument gingerly, as though it might explode.

"He's swearing again," he explained, sadly, in answer to Gordon's look of inquiry. "He wants to know when I am going to stop running away from the wire. He has a stack of messages to send, he says, but I guess he'd better wait and take your copy first; don't you think so?"

"Yes, I do," said Gordon. "I don't want any more messages than I've had. That's the best I can do," he said, as he threw his manuscript down beside Stedman. "And they can keep on cabling until the wire burns red hot, and they won't get any more."

There was silence in the office for some time, while Stedman looked over Gordon's copy, and Gordon stared dejectedly out at the ocean.

"This is pretty poor stuff, Gordon," said Stedman. "It's like giving people milk when they want brandy."

"Don't you suppose I know that?" growled Gordon. "It's the best I can do, isn't it? It's not my fault that we are not all dead now. I can't massacre foreign residents if there are no foreign residents, but I can commit suicide, though, and I'll do it if something don't happen."

There was a long pause, in which the silence of

the office was only broken by the sound of the waves beating on the coral reefs outside. Stedman raised his head wearily.

"He's swearing again," he said; "he says this stuff of yours is all nonsense. He says stock in the Y. C. C. has gone up to one hundred and two, and that owners are unloading and making their fortunes, and that this sort of descriptive writing is not what the company want."

"What's he think I'm here for?" cried Gordon. "Does he think I pulled down the German flag and risked my neck half a dozen times and had myself made King just to boom his Yokohama cable stock? Confound him! You might at least swear back. Tell him just what the situation is in a few words. Here, stop that rigmarole to the paper, and explain to your home office that we are awaiting developments, and that, in the meanwhile, they must put up with the best we can send them. Wait; send this to Octavia."

Gordon wrote rapidly, and read what he wrote as rapidly as it was written.

"Operator, Octavia. You seem to have misunderstood my first message. The facts in the case are these. A German man-of-war raised a flag on this island. It was pulled down and the American flag raised in its place and saluted by a brass cannon. The German man-of-war fired once at the flag and knocked it down, and then steamed away and has not been seen since. Two huts were upset, that is all the damage done; the battery consisted of the one brass cannon before mentioned. No one, either native or foreign, has been massacred. The English residents are two sailors. The American residents are the young man who is sending you this cable and myself. Our first message was quite true in substance, but perhaps misleading in detail. I made it so because I fully expected much more to happen immediately. Nothing has happened, or seems likely to happen, and that is the exact situation up to date. Albert Gordon."

"Now," he asked, after a pause, "what does he say to that?"

"He doesn't say anything," said Stedman.

"I guess he has fainted. Here it comes," he added in the same breath. He bent toward his instrument, and Gordon raised himself from his chair and stood beside him as he read it off. The two young men hardly breathed in the intensity of their interest.

"Dear Stedman," he slowly read aloud. "You and your young friend are a couple of fools. If you had allowed me to send you the messages awaiting transmission here to you, you would not have sent me such a confession of guilt as you have just done. You had better leave Opeki at once or hide in the hills. I am afraid I have placed you in a somewhat compromising position with the company, which is unfortunate, especially as, if I am not mistaken, they owe you some back pay. You should have been wiser in your day, and bought Y. C. C. stock when it was down to five cents, as 'yours truly' did. You are not, Stedman, as bright a boy as some. And as for your friend, the war-correspondent, he has queered himself for life. You see, my dear Stedman, after I had sent off your first message, and demands for further details came pouring in, and I could not get you at the wire to supply them, I took the liberty of sending some on myself."

"Great Heavens!" gasped Gordon.

Stedman grew very white under his tan, and the perspiration rolled on his cheeks.

"Your message was so general in its nature, that it allowed my imagination full play, and I sent on what I thought would please the papers, and, what was much more important to me, would advertise the Y. C. C. stock. This I have been doing while waiting for material from you. Not having a clear idea of the dimensions or population of Opeki, it is possible that I have done you and your news-

Made Himself King

And in front of these, a clumsy fishing-boat rose and fell on each passing wave. Two sailors sat in the stern, holding the rope and tiller, and in the bow, with their backs turned forever toward Ope-ki, stood two young boys, their faces lit by the glow of the setting sun and stirred by the sight of the great engines of war plunging past them on their errand of vengeance.

"Stedman," said the elder boy, in an awe-struck whisper, and with a wave of his hand, "we have not lived in vain."